Z:

One Family's Journey from Immigration Through Poverty to the Fulfillment of the Promise of America

K. Adrian Zonneville

ISBN: **1717399029**
ISBN-13: **978-1717399021**

DEDICATION

This book is dedicated to Martinus and Suzanne Zonneville for having the courage and spirit to board a very cold, dank ship with a hundred dollars in their pockets to begin a new life for all of us in America. Without their willingness to begin anew we would not have the lives we have lived. We are forever in your debt.

CONTENTS

ACKNOWLEDGMENTS

This book does not happen without the aid of the Zonneville family. They contributed pictures and love and need to be thanked. To Betsy and Bob, Robin and Manette, David and Cindy, my siblings and their spouses. To all the nieces and nephews, cousins, children and grandchildren who keep this family chugging along. To my mother, Carol A. Zonneville, my children Kathryn and Adrienne my undying thanks, you are my heart. To my father, Robert E. Zonneville, the subject of this book for living a life worth writing about and inspiring all around you. To Elvyra for keeping him young and on his toes. But mostly to the person who makes my life worth living and the reason I continue to try and become a better person, my wife, love and friend, Mumford!

With an Edit assist from Vern Morrison, Susanne Wilson and the lovely Ms. Mumford

Great occasions do not make heroes or cowards. They simply unveil them to the eyes of men. Silently and imperceptibly, as we wake or sleep, we grow strong or week, and at last some crisis shows us what we have become. Brooke Foss Westcott

FOREWORD

Z. That was what everyone called him. Oh, a few called him Bob, one guy called him Robert and if you worked for him, it was Mr. Z. But those who knew him, those who were close, they called him Z. It just seemed to fit. It said it all. We used to think it was because Zonneville was too hard for them to wrap their heads around. "It's like a Bonneville car only with a Z!" we would explain. Oh, Zonnerville, or Zoneville they would try. Nope, Z.

There was even an enterprising car salesman in the mid-60's who was willing to change all the B's on a Pontiac Bonneville to Zs if my Dad would go the extra couple hundred bucks up from the Safari wagon. We were quite disappointed when my dad turned him down.

He has always been bigger than life. You don't outshine him even when he is sitting quietly out of the way. It is not as if he tries to be the center of attention, I don't think he actually needs to be admired or adored; he just is. There is just so much life in the man, even at 93 years old, it spills out of him. He is, like all in our family, loud and abrasive, crude but not offensive, funny and immortal. He just can't be stopped.

His hand writing is atrocious. Trust me. I am the keeper of the notes and I feel like I need someone who has worked as a cryptographer just to get through a simple sentence. He was known for that handwriting. When he was an assistant manager of Associated Transport he walked through dispatch one time and found a Hostess cupcake on somebody's desk, picked it up and took a bite. "Hey Mr. Z, that ain't yours!" yelled the offended party. "Yeah it is," calmly explained my father, "look it has my name written right on top." Those of the proper age and upbringing will understand that without further explanation.

He asked me to write this for him. I said, 'like an autobiography?"

"No, write it like you. If you write it like I'm writing it then it sounds like I'm bragging and I'm not bragging just lucky. These are just the facts."

My father was always happy to explain that he, Robert Earl Zonneville, was truly the luckiest man to ever live. He might have been but sometimes we make our own luck as well. It is his personality, his life, his zest and gusto, his giving, his caring that draws people to him, that make them care for him. They know his word is his bond. Contracts mean nothing, if you won't keep your word what good is a piece of paper. If Z says it, believe it.

This is what he gave me to begin this journey;

"It was June 1992 and my wife and I were driving from Mentor Ohio to Williamson, NY, my hometown. It was the Fiftieth High School reunion of the Class of '42. A four and half hour drive but the weather was pleasant, the reunion wasn't until the next day and I had never missed a Reunion!

Of the Class of 1942 one schoolmate had been killed during World War Two and several others had passed over the years. It was, after all, a Fiftieth Reunion. Time passes and so do our friends and family. Yet a high percentage still remained and many lived close by

Williamson, it would be a good turnout.

The Reunion was to be held at the golf club in Sodus Point, NY, as Williamson was a dry town and we definitely were not. After cocktails and dinner, I had the honor to make a few comments. Before my own comments I was fortunate to introduce our former High School principal, Grant Northrup. We were very lucky he was still alive and well enough to attend from his home in Atlanta, where he had retired after serving as president of a collage.

He stated, "I am not going to give a speech but instead would rather read you a letter."

He had not read more than a few lines when my wife leaned over and asked, "Are you alright?"

"I wrote that letter."

Christmas Eve-1944
Somewhere in Germany

Hello Mr. Northrup,

Tonight I received a Christmas package from my mother and enclosed was a copy of the school newspaper, so I decided to write you a few lines. I thought the paper was very good and it brought back many happy memories of my high school days. I often times wish I were back there and had it all to do over again. Since coming in to the Army I have found many times that I passed some very good opportunities while in high school.

Since leaving the states a little over a year ago I have visited several European countries that only a couple years back were merely spots on a map. In some cases I have seen some very beautiful sights and in other cases they were sights of utter destruction caused by the ruthlessness of war.

Often times when I see the latter of these two, I wonder if man is as civilized as we are supposed to be or if we are still barbarians. I often wonder why, when these controversial subjects arise, that they couldn't just as well be settled in a civilized way; at a peace table or something similar to that. Maybe the future will bear this out.

Well Mr. Northrup, everything is fine here and I hope you are well also. Things are pretty quiet up here tonight and it sure seems good. Right now there are five of us up in a German foxhole. It is one they sort of evacuated a short time ago, so we moved in to enjoy its comforts. Jerry is starting to throw some shells at us now so I guess I better sign off.

Sincerely yours,

Bob

As he finished his reading he presented me the letter stating, "I have made a copy for myself, you should have this."

"Grant," I replied, "I am surprised you would keep a letter from me. I was a bit of a handful back in high school."

He smiled, "You were always one of my favorites because of your energy and you just seemed to like everybody. But you WERE a handful at times."

The following day on our ride back home Carol, my wife, said to me, "Bob, after hearing that letter and all at the reunion and thinking about all you have done and the life you have led, why don't you write a book about your life?"

That started the thinking."

My wife and I were driving home from skiing in upstate New York when my phone buzzed. It was my father's number. We were actually on our way to his home for dinner to celebrate his 93rd birthday. Why would he be calling? I assumed he had forgotten something needed for the dinner, and knowing I was on my way, he wanted us to drive by the grocery store. That is what sons are for: Change the channel! Hold the left antenna up just a bit, now pull the right one forward, perfect! No, hold that so I can watch the game. 'Swing by the store' was a piece of cake. We were only about an hour out.

I should stop to explain something; my father and I spent our lives on the road, he with trucking, me with entertainment, so to us an hour out is around the corner. For my father to call me when I was almost there was curious. To be perfectly honest he rarely forgot anything, he leaves nothing to chance but, then again, well, he was turning 93!

He was calling to ask me a favor. There is nothing in this world I would not do for my father. He is the finest man I have ever known. He is constant, abrasive, loud, overbearing, giving to a fault and generous. He always asks never demands, though I hear the steel in the request.

Our family, friends, and many of his longtime business associates had been pushing and prodding him for the past twenty-five years to write a book on his life. His father had arrived from Holland with next to nothing. He had been born dirt poor and grown up in the depression. He served in WWII landing on Omaha beach in June of 1944. He made it back home intact, a bit banged up but loaded down with medals. He then married, raised a family, succeeded in his love, trucking, and had been married for 61 years until Mom passed. He returned to college, refusing the free auditing of classes offered by the state of Ohio because he wanted his diploma. So, he paid for his classes, graduated, on the dean's list, remarried a lovely woman named Elvyra, and gives most every moment to someone or some charity, anyone, who needs him. That's my Dad in a nutshell. When you delve into detail the story is truly amazing and inspiring. When I was a kid I remember reading in a science magazine about the search for perpetual motion and I thought, they should meet my dad. Still true at 93.

"You've written a book, published and written a bunch of songs, right?" he began, "I need you to do me a favor."

I couldn't believe my dad would ask me what I knew was coming.

"I just can't get this going. Everyone told me it was almost impossible to write about yourself but I thought I could. But it just sounds wrong, like you're full of yourself and that ain't right," he continues, "so, I want to know if you would write the book."

Plain simple, no beating around any bushes-oh, sure, he might drive over them or push them out of the way, but that is my father. "Of course, I will," I said, calm as a cucumber. I knew I'd need to push every other project I have to the back of the line. I also knew I would be overjoyed to do so.

My hands began to shake as soon as I pushed the button to hang up the phone. Was I insane? The responsibility weighed on me as if I was Atlas without the strength. This was not just a book about my father but about my family. Really, it was a book about my country. If there was ever a personification of America and her promise fulfilled, it was my father.

My wife had been listening in on the call and looked at me with a bit of admiration. "That is so cool he wants you to do this," says she, without a hint of sarcasm or understanding of what this will entail. I'll give my wife this, she has this unreasoned, irrefutable and totally unwarranted belief that I can do just about anything. My father's fault, as he always believed, was that if you could baffle them with BS then you would find a way once you had time to think. And he filled me with that same erroneous confidence. Yeah, right! I can do anything if I believe hard enough. Look Tinker Bell lives! That is stuff I sell and she is my best customer.

Is my father special? Yeah, he's my dad. But beyond that, I don't know. He is the American dream personified, and yet his story has been told a thousand different ways by millions of others who also defined the spirit and the promise of this country.

And yet, I think he is more. He is the son and grandson of people who pulled up their roots and left their family behind to begin a new-life, a new chapter, hell, a whole new book in the family. They came with next to nothing but hope. They were poor, though they never realized it, because when you are poor surrounded by others who are just as poor, you are average.

They came to escape forced service in the military, and within his grandfather's life my father would return to the homeland to fight a war to end tyranny. He would be wounded twice and he witnessed unbelievable horrors, and he witnessed scenes of great beauty and the kindness of the human spirit. He would liberate concentration camps of skeletons and then come home to begin life again as one of the kindest, most generous people on the planet. Maybe he thought he could make up for some of humanities cruelty.

The family had successes and failures, financially and personally, losing their land, their children and their money, but they never lost their dreams. It seems to live in the DNA. He would become through sheer will, the love of an industry, and a yearning to learn and improve his lot in life, someone who was considered to be the most knowledgeable and top man in his business. When he retired the first time he was the president of a major trucking company. His brothers were blessed as well with vocations they loved and children who continued the tradition by following their own dreams.

My father and his brothers never pressured their children to follow in their footsteps when it came time t decide how to make a living, but they did encourage their children to follow their dreams. They also encouraged them to understand you had to work hard and put up with a lot of crap from some people, but if you believed in yourself and didn't quit, you stood a good chance of achieving those dreams. As my father once told me, "if you do something you love, if you do something not for the money but because you couldn't wait to go to work every day, you will never work a day in your life." We have been lucky.

So, is my dad special? You bet your ass he is! It is with great trepidation, pride, love and honor that I present to you Robert E. Zonneville.

Beginning a New Life

Where does the life of a family begin? Where does its history commence? If there are no records to be found does history begin at memory? With the passing of time and people how short or long can our history be? Does it begin in the old country? What if no one talks of the old country? What if there has been consensual amnesia?

In our family, no one speaks of the Old Country; it was a place to leave. We do not talk about unpleasant things, and it was unpleasant or why would we be here? If we wanted to remain Dutch, we would have remained in Holland. We are Americans. This is where life begins.

That was the attitude of my grandparents. We live here now, we are Americans. You will speak English in this house when you visit, or don't come. We left Holland, now we leave all that is Dutch behind. That was their frame of mind. My grandfather's brothers would come over and only wish to speak Dutch. He told them, "in this house you speak American." So they stopped coming. And if Grandpa Adrian wished to see them he could go to their houses where they still spoke Dutch. Grandpa's brother Jacob had never learned the language. He'd been older than the rest when their parents had loaded on a ship to come to this country. It was harder for him and easier for his younger siblings. The young are like sponges: they soak in anything put in front of them, especially if the parents are supportive. So, they still spoke mostly Dutch at Jacob's house.

And though my father asked again and again about Holland, the Old Country, they said nothing, there was nothing to say about it. They left. Throughout their lives they saw nothing constructive about bringing up misery. My Grandfather was young when he left, only nine years old, and he did not bring good memories with him, at least none he cared to share. All he remembered was his parents did not believe in war or the military, and in Holland you served, whether you cared for it or not. So they left for a better life here. That was everything my father needed to know. He would never learn a word of Dutch.

They sold what they had, bought steerage on a ship, and they never looked back. Whether that was true or not only my grandfather would know and would say no more. They suffered a winter crossing of the Atlantic-cold, heavy waves and sea sickness, the horrors of cross-oceanic travel in the early part of the last century for the poor, the tired, the unwashed masses.

They came to America to raise a family, farm, live and die. Till the soil, bake fresh bread, learn the language and the ways of this country. Become educated: that was the way to get ahead in this world and hope your children would do better. It was worth the sacrifice. We are Americans.

February 23, 1907, the S.S. Potsdam left Rotterdam bound for New York. According to the ships manifest, among the passengers listed were, Martinus Johannus Zonneville, born May 5, 1867 in Hoofdplaat, (the son of Adriaan Zonneville, born October 3, 1815 in Biervliet, and Suzanne Boone, born June 13, 1824 in Hoofdplaat) and Suzanne (DeBatz) Zonneville, born in Schoondijke in 1869. They were accompanied by their four children; Jacob, aged 19, Adrian, aged 9, Isaac aged 4 and their only daughter Suzanne, the baby, aged 2.

To start their new life, they carried with them their entire fortune of one hundred dollars. That meager sum would now have to finance all their hopes and dreams. On March 6, 1907 they arrived at Ellis Island in New York, frightened, tired, sick from the voyage and wanting to feel the land beneath them. It was time to find good dirt and their new home.

They made their way to Wayne County in upstate New York, near the Williamson-Sodus area. There was family there, those who had come before. Extended family, distant cousins and friends of Old World friends, but family nonetheless, as well as others from Holland. Others who had come from the Old Country and still spoke the language; and their children who could speak both American and Dutch, and thus could act as interpreters. It would help the family ease into this new world. It was a cocoon to wrap themselves in until they could assimilate. A place to feel safe and protected while they learned the new rules and the new language.

Martin and Suzanne either begged or borrowed money from relatives and the Dutch community, or received a land contract, no one ever really knew, so they could purchase a small fruit farm on the Bear Swamp Road in Williamson, New York. That was how it was done in the early part of the last century. People would come to the new world, settle with others from the Old Country, and they, in turn, would help them finance their dream. No brick and mortar banks, just informal associations of fellow immigrants lending a hand. They grew and harvested apples, peaches and cherries and, by all accounts, were successful enough not to go hungry.

The two youngest boys, Adrian and Isaac, attended the local school for several years where they became proficient at English. Their elder brother Jacob never bothered to learn English, except for a few words and phrases to get by. Either he found it too difficult or he was just unwilling to learn the new language. He chose only to speak Dutch, leading to the friction within the family later in life.

Adjusting to a new life in a new world was difficult enough, and shortly after they had set up house in Williamson, Suzanne suddenly died, prompting the others to discuss for the first and only time the question of whether or not to return to Holland. Did they want to stay and be reminded of this tragedy every day of their lives? The discussion was a brief one; they chose to remain in their new home. Returning to Holland would not bring her back and would only bring more heartache and sorrow with the failure of beginning a new life.

The life of the farmer doesn't change much. There are good years and bad. You are either too cold, too hot, too wet and too dry. You know sorrow and joy. You sow and you reap. You plant your crops, you care for them, you harvest them. You prune the trees, you pick the fruit, you go to market. Days become weeks, become months, become years, and you hardly notice the sun rising and setting. You don't see the new wrinkles filling your face, the brown hair on your head becoming grey, then becoming white. Before you notice the hair on their chins and voices that have traded the squeak of puberty for the resonance of adults, the children have become adults and are moving out on their own. It is the way of life.

The Zonnevilles didn't travel or see exciting sights, never taking the opportunity to explore and see this new land. They never saw more than their own farm and surrounding farms. They would go into town from time to time, but they were not extravagant in their lives or taste. There would no great highs, or truly devastating lows. They never seemed to need more than they could find within a few miles from the family farm.

There isn't the time nor the financial resources for travel and discovery when you are a farmer, scratching your existence from the soil. They endured and raised the family and loved and were thankful for all they had. Simple lives aren't exciting, but they can be quite rewarding at the end of the day. This was not uncommon for families of the era. Only the rich could afford to travel or take time for leisure. The working classes earned their title-they worked. Usually seven days a week and for very low wages. It wasn't until the advent of the labor unions in the 1920's and 1930's that the middle class was birthed. And it was a painful and bloody birthing.

On March 22, 1922 Adrian moved out of family home to begin his new life with his new wife, Mattie Leona Shippers. They would follow in the family tradition and farm and raise children and fruit.

Very quickly they had a daughter, Evelyn, but as was common at the time she survived for less than a year. Infant mortality at the beginning of the twentieth century was high, ranging seventy to eighty per thousand. They were not alone in their sorrow; many families had carried tiny coffins to graveyards. Though heartbreaking it was not unexpected. His grandparents had lost two children either at birth or very young. His parents lost three of their six children, all girls, before any of the girls could attain their third birthday.

My father entered the world on January 23, 1925. Shortly after my father joined the Zonneville clan, kicking and screaming, giving some indication of what the future would hold, Adrian and Mattie set down roots on a forty-acre fruit farm down the Bear Swamp Road from his parents. They begged, borrowed and promised the money for a down payment. The banks wouldn't help a young family just starting out, so the Dutch community helped each other once again, lending start-up venture to new families so they might get a start on life. It was 1925. Adrian and Mattie now had a newborn, healthy baby boy, a new farm and they had each other; life was filled with promise and hope.

On May 29, 1926 Duane, a big, strapping, healthy baby boy joined the family. Another beautiful daughter, Muriel, came along in 1928 but she only survived for six months. Richard was born on November 2, 1931 and right on his heels on October 7, 1932 was Allen. Adrian and Mattie had one more son, Gerald, in 1935 but like his sisters before him did not survive, lasting a mere two months. It was a time of extreme highs and lows for the young family, but strength comes from adversity.

They farmed apples and peaches to sell, and they set aside several acres for their own use as a vegetable garden. The home, though comfortable, had no electricity or indoor plumbing, and only one large register in the center room for heating. No heat found its' way to the second-floor bedrooms, so heavy quilts were a must in the cold northern New York winters.

Farm work is arduous labor driven by muscle and determination. For the heavy lifting they had George and Dan, two good, solid workhorses, a must on any working homestead. They also had a few cows, some pigs and they raised chickens. So, the only necessities they needed to go to town for and purchase were flour, sugar and spices. It was a hard life, but a good one. They were lucky as they also had an icebox for refrigeration. This is not to be confused with a refrigerator, with its mechanics and cooling systems, and powered by electricity, no, this was an insulated box they would put ice in. The ice was either delivered by the iceman or cut from the ponds out on the farms when funds were low, to keep their food cold.

On cold winter mornings they would literally hop out of bed and run to the kitchen, clothes in hand, to get dressed by the old iron kitchen stove. Warmth as well as delicious smells always emanated from the stove, filling the kitchen and spilling out into the rest of the house. Well, the smells made it upstairs, but the warmth did not! A home cooked breakfast of bread, eggs and potatoes was enough incentive to roust any child from a cold bed.

Their home was always filled with the aroma of fresh baked bread, pies, canning and cooking meats and vegetables. It was an aroma that permeated the house and escaped out the kitchen door and into the surrounding yard. Delicious! Years later we would run from the car into that aroma.

Of course, the freezing temperatures and howling wind made a trip to the outhouse an adventure. One did not waste time reading the Sears catalogue, but one could and did use it for another purpose. And I'll leave that to your imagination.

The farm on Bear Swamp Road, where dad learned the trade, was just down the way from his grandparents' farm as well as just up the road from his Uncle Jacob's. The area was quickly becoming Zonneville Central. This was not uncommon for the time. Sons and daughters would marry and purchase land close to the family homestead, so all could continue to help each other and share in the labor and the bounty. It was a built-in support system; parents were there for their children who were there for their children who were there for their elders. You relied on each other as family and friend and you could rely on friends to be there when family couldn't.

Bear Swamp Road, like most farm roads of the era, a dirt lane. It was muddy when it rained all through the spring, hard and dusty in the summer and almost impassable in the winter. Upstate New York sits on the edge of Lake Ontario and catches the west winds off Lake Erie. So, no matter which way the wind blows snow will come. And when it comes, it comes by the foot, swirling and leaving drifts on the roads, drifts which can reach five feet high and more. Given that many people at the time still used horses for transport and pulling wagons and it would mean up to a week, sometimes, without being able to leave the house. And when you finally could travel, what with spring rains and muddy roads, well, between horse hooves and wagon wheels the ruts were deep and the holes were plentiful and unavoidable. It made for rough riding and unpleasant travel but that was the way of life; there was no highway department to come and fill the pot holes and grade the roads.

Money, always tight for those who work the land, got tighter as years passed for the young Zonneville family. They had arrived in America with only a hundred dollars in Martin's pockets and none In Adrian's. Factor in that no one farms to become rich, add in the loss of three children within a relatively short period of time, doctor and burial bills, and you arrive at poor. Doctors weren't outrageously expensive for the time, but money is relative. A hundred dollars to a millionaire is a drop in the bucket, a hundred dollars to a young family who recently purchased a farm and now had four sons to support is the entire bucket.

Harvest is what all farmers work towards. Until then it is all borrowed money, hard work, early, early mornings and long days without reward, only promise. You get your income for the year when the crop comes in and you can sell to distributors or at market. It is what all wait and hope for. Good crop, good year, and you don't have to go deep into debt borrowing for the next year. Bad crop, bad year and deep hole to climb out of. Hope: it is the farmers life.

October 29, 1929. A date that will always live in financial history. The Great Crash and the official date of the start of the Great Depression. Most people discuss how this affected Wall Street and the high rollers and wealthy. They talk about the massive amount of wealth lost that day. They very seldom focus in on how this affected the common man, the farmer, the laborer, the fella just trying to keep a roof over the heads of his family and food on the table.

Oh, they'd talk about it and show the soup lines and the unemployment lines in the movies, but to those like my grandfather and his brothers and father, it would be devastating. Families were torn apart; men died from the shame of not having the ability to take care of those they loved and cherished. Proud men begged for nickels or sold what they had for a pittance in the hopes of putting food on the table for their families one more time. It was heartbreaking, spirit sucking, and soul destroying for those who had nothing and now were forced to either move elsewhere, leaving families behind in the hopes of finding work, or just abandoning hope, family and life.

Farm prices dropped quickly and consistently. What they grew was becoming worth less and less every day. The farm, the land, itself wasn't worth much and certainly no longer worth what my grandfather paid for it a few years earlier. Times got harder, money got tighter, and the work got harsher for less and less return.

During all this my father started school in 1930 at the Jersey Schoolhouse, a one room school encompassing kindergarten through eighth grade all packed in a tiny room, each row of chairs denoting a specific grade. Students who went passed eighth grade were bussed to a separate high school in Williamson, central to all surrounding areas, combining several towns and villages into one school.

Jersey School was typical of the community buildings at the time with no indoor plumbing, a stove for heating, no electricity and, of course, an outhouse. These schools were situated around the county in such a way that students only had to walk about a mile and a half each way to and from home. Remember they were five to thirteen years old at the time. In the depths of winter, kids had to walk through deep snow drifts, both ways, uphill, and, wow, I guess some of those stories were true after all.

In the 1930's Williamson decided to centralize their school districts. They closed down the one room schoolhouses and began bussing children to the Williamson Central School. This new edifice had central heating, indoor plumbing, electricity, a gym and an auditorium for plays and such. I asked my dad, "Wasn't that a bit intimidating, frightening and terrifying to move from a one room schoolhouse, where you knew everyone in the building, to a much larger place filled with hundreds of kids you'd never had any interaction with?"

He laughed, "are you kidding? We were going from a bare-knuckle shack with no indoor plumbing or electricity to a modern building filled with all the amenities you could want. And there were new kids to meet every time you turned around! It was exciting and brought new experiences and friendships every day!"

And there you have the essence of my father. One of the great lessons I learned--and there have been many--was there are no strangers in this world, just folks he hadn't had the chance to meet yet. I found it eye opening that he had been this way since a small child. I guess some traits are ingrained in the DNA rather than learned.

I believe if they had known what the Taj Mahal was they would've believed they had been transported to go to school there. Quite a jump up the social ladder. Though getting to and from remained an arduous and remarkable experience.

Keep in mind even though they rode in buses, the roads were those same dirt roads, pocked and rutted by horses and wagons, mud bogs in the spring, and ice and snow covered in the winter; and bus suspension was almost nonexistent. The buses were hot in the late spring and early autumn and freezing in the winter. Heat and air conditioning? We'll invent that in the future. Not a very pleasant ride but far superior to walking the long distance into town and back home. Well, most of the time.

The desks at the new school were equipped, as all were in this time, with inkwells. These were in the top right-hand corner of the desk, they were filled with ink so students could dip their pens and write.

Well, as he entered the fourth grade filled with confidence and the devil, young Robert Zonneville noted a blond girl with the prettiest curls sitting in front of him. He thought it would be funny of he dunked these lovely blond curls in the inkwell. He did. It wasn't. The ink dripped and spilled on her dress, ruining it. By the time he made it home, the girls' parents had called his parents to report the incident and to demand payment for the dress. Of course, his folks, though hard up for living expenses as it was, had to find the money.

He mentioned that he was severely reprimanded. I believe that was code for a whooping that allowed him to stand for meals for a length of time; approximately the amount of time it took to earn the money to pay them back. You broke it, you bought it and we expect payment in full. He would find a way.

1935 saw the final straw land on the camels' back and his folks lost the farm. Prices for produce no longer covered the cost of growing it. They didn't bother to harvest most of the fruit and vegetables as the cost of harvesting would only serve to increase their losses. They would have to leave the farm and find somewhere new to live.

Somehow, somewhere my grandfather found the money to purchase a very used truck, so he could transport produce grown by other farmers to New York City and Philadelphia. If he couldn't grow it himself, he could damn well stay involved in farming by helping others while helping his own family. Large cities, no matter how hard hit by the economic collapse and following depression, still did not have the ability nor the land to produce what they consumed, so if you could get the produce to them, prices were much better for the farmers and the haulers.

The family was now renting a home in Williamson for twelve dollars a month. It was not the farm-which had been heartbreaking and embarrassing for his father to lose, though many others were paddling the same canoe, in the same dry streambed-but they could now easily walk to school.

But the greatest gifts sometimes come from the darkest days. During summer vacations, uncle Duane and my dad got to tag along with their father to help load and unload the truck. You can imagine what a magical and wondrous experience this was for a couple of small-town hick children from upstate New York, afforded the opportunity to visit two of the grandest cities in the country. They must have thought they had traveled to a whole new world: one filled with skyscrapers, massive concrete buildings, cars and trucks whizzing by at forty miles an hour. And people, tens of thousands of people, everywhere they looked. One cannot even imagine the awe that defined their features; one would assume they walked, looking but without focusing, pointing over here and there, at this person or those. And always staring skyward in wonder at these impossibly tall buildings. Two adolescent boys, mouths agape and staring at all the wonders of the modern world laid out before them. Appearing for all the world to see: the rural farm boy come to the big city and in awe of civilization and the modern world.

Life is For The Living

1935 was a very bad year. Not only did Adrian and Mattie lose their farm, but they also lost their new baby, Gerald. Poverty takes many forms and it seemed that 1935 somehow wanted to make sure they knew intimately each and every facet of it.

There is the poverty of money which bottoms out at nothing. You can't go lower. When there is nothing, there is nothing to take, nothing to lose. You can only owe more but there comes a time when that number loses all meaning. That is poverty, and that was my family in 1935.

There is the poverty of soul, when you lose what truly matters to you. The family had lost two daughters previously; they knew the heartbreak. To lose Gerald less two months into life was devastating. The money owed for doctors and such just added to the height of the mountain of sorrow and debt. They'd lost the farm and started the new trucking business, they'd gone for broke, and made it. It was now time to go for more.

There is the poverty of hope. As far as I can ascertain, this is not in the Zonneville lexicon. I have never seen it in any member of the family. I have never even heard it mentioned, certainly not by my father. And I have never witnessed anyone in this family face any adversity without, at the very least, the outward façade of determination and a visceral belief that somehow, some way, everything would work out. Maybe not exactly the way they wanted, but they would survive and thrive.

And there is the poverty of opportunity. Many suffer from this even today. They see no way forward, no way to begin, let alone to succeed in any way, and therefore they throw in the towel. We do not seem to have that in our DNA. Maybe we're just too dumb to know when to quit or too stupid to realize something is impossible, but Zonnevilles bull their way through to, at the minimum, break even. Even when common sense screams to stop, turn, go back, we just don't seem to have the smarts. From what I have been able to determine, what I thought was just a malfunction in my closest relatives really has been pervasive throughout the family for generations. No matter how low he and his family were laid, my grandfather believed, and he made everyone else believe. So, they persevered, and all put a shoulder to life's wheel, and they pushed.

My grandfather was a great believer in the notion that if you wanted something, you worked for it. Life didn't give you anything except the chance to get up each day, take another breath, and work a little harder towards whatever goal you could see down the road. I cannot ever remember any of the old folks, the aunts and uncles, my grandfather or Hazel (I'll explain her later), nor especially my parents, idly wishing or dreaming of riches and wealth. They never spoke of leisure. There were things they enjoyed—golf, vacations to Canada, a beer at the tavern, time with friends and family—but they never mentioned lounging about while servants waited on them. Work was a given, leisure was to be enjoyed in small measure.

There was no money, so the concept of an allowance in my grandfather's house was as foreign as Greek. He did not understand the concept of paying your children for work they should be doing because they were part of the family. If you needed money for some bauble or a bike or whatever you dreamt up, there were plenty of hours in the day that you had nothing to do; get a job.

The closest city to Williamson was Rochester, New York, and they had two daily newspapers: The Democrat and Chronicle in the morning and the Times-Union in the afternoon. Dad and his brother Duane managed to finagle routes on The Democrat and Chronicle. This was ideal, as they both loved to play sports and wished to participate in other afterschool activities. The morning paper afforded them the opportunity to both work and play.

Both Dad and Duane had approximately forty-five to fifty customers each. They made one cent from each daily paper, for which the customer paid three cents, and two cents from the Sunday paper, for which the customer paid ten cents. So if they could get all to sign up for all seven days they would make a whopping eight cents per week per customer or, for those of you without proper math skills, $3.50-$4.00 per week!

They had the job, now all they needed to do was find a way to appropriate a bicycle for each to do that job. They arrived at the local hardware store hats in hand, trying to make a deal. They had to now convince the store owner to trust them to pay him one dollar each week—both guaranteeing if one didn't pay, the other would—if he would sell them each a bike. They swore on all that was holy, as well as their mother and their eternal souls, they would fulfill this contract. If they were to fail, he would have slave labor from these two charmers for a year. Either these two young smoothies were very fast talkers, or the store owner called their father as a secondary guarantor, but either way they got the bikes, and they were in business.

As school days came to a close each summer, it afforded them the chance to find more work in their now-ample spare time. So, once again Duane and Dad, as the eldest brothers, would pick up their papers as soon as they were delivered to the distribution point, race through their appointed rounds, and then wander the fields picking wild strawberries, blackberries, blueberries, whatever was available. They would then turn around and sell the berries for five to ten cents a quart. All profit for enterprising young boys willing to bust their butts.

As they got older they were able to hire on to farms weeding carrots all summer vacation. They crawled up and down rows of carrots on their hands and knees, trying to weed a couple rows each pass. They worked ten-hour days, with an hour for lunch, and were paid the kingly sum of fifteen cents an hour, or a dollar-fifty per day. If it rained or there was any other kind of interruption from the heavens or Earth, that time lost was deducted from their pay.

Promise began to take root in 1940. Things were looking up. My grandparents had saved a little money—nickels and dimes do add up after a while. The trucking business had gotten them through the toughest times and made it possible for them to once again return to the land. They were able to purchase a small farm outside of Williamson. Time to move once again from the town to the farm. They would return to their roots and the life they loved.

They were, once again, immersed in agrarian bliss. They woke to the sounds of chickens in the yard, cows in the field, and pigs in the sty. Of course, that meant early rising to milk the cows, feed the chickens, and slop the pigs before they set off to paper routes. They would scurry home for a quick breakfast, wash up, and get ready for school. After school, if there were no activities they had to show up for, they would head back home and do chores. If there were sports and such, they would practice and then head home, knowing the chores would be there, waiting patiently. Their father continued the trucking business, though on a more part-time level, as the extra income helped keep the farm afloat in the early years. And he found he could easily do both, and if you had the time you filled it with something productive. There is nothing more productive than work, now is there? He had learned from his previous loss to get ahead and stay ahead of the market and the bankers.

Time and life do not remain in stasis for anyone. All was going well in 1941, the farm doing well, the family healthy and prospering in their little world, until one winter morning.

My father was delivering his papers in the cold pre-dawn dark. The weather had turned ugly with wind and blowing snow. He couldn't see more than a few feet in front of him, but he knew the route. He could do it blindfolded, and it seemed that would come in handy on this blustery morn. The car coming from the opposite direction could not see the young man on the bicycle, and the bicyclist never saw the car until it was too late.

Someone from Young's Funeral Home came to pick him up, as they provided the ambulance service for the area. They thought he would not last the trip but took him to the hospital in Sodus, New York. His mother, who'd been brought by the police to her son's side, wept for her dying child the whole way. I cannot imagine what that must have felt like for her. She'd lost three children in their infancy and now her eldest lay in an ambulance, with all involved believing he hadn't a chance at survival.

A few days later he awoke, slowly coming back to consciousness. The nurse on duty ran to find Dr. Robert Harris, his attending physician (and coincidentally one of his customers on the newspaper route).

"Do you know where you are?" the doctor asked while staring hard to read my father's face, searching his eyes for response.

My Dad replied he had no idea.

"You have been in a very serious accident," the doctor told him, "and are very lucky to be alive."

My Dad, like all mid-teenaged boys with the intelligence of a goat, tried to get out of the hospital bed.

"You are strapped to this bed," Dr. Harris explained sternly, "and will remain that way for the next thirty days. You're busted up pretty good, with enough broken bones for a lifetime, and you're scraped and bloodied over most of your body. What's more, your skull has been fractured in three places. That driver must've hit you dead on to break that head," he smiled. "We'll try to get you sitting up, slowly, inch by inch, in a month. Until then, you lay still."

So for the next month my father ate blended foods through one straw and drank water through another. Small-town communities are more than a few families sharing a common region. They are communities in the deepest sense of the word. Many are, in fact, family; the rest are people you have known your entire life. Families intermarry, go to church together, help plant and harvest, share the soil and life, and so it was with my father's community.

His friends and fellow students, some of whom he knew only in passing, came around to the hospital to keep him company, to break up the mind-numbing boredom, and to help him keep up his school work. His teachers came by after school to tutor him, so he missed nothing and did not fall behind. I know you're wondering: wasn't that cruel and unusual punishment to bring school to the hospital? Not for him. Anyone as active physically, mentally, and congenially as my father would go stir crazy within days of being strapped motionless to a bed. These visits were what kept him active and engaged and kept his spirits from flagging. It was as necessary a medicine as anything the doctors and nurses might be giving him.

And because of all the hard work by this community he was able to pass to the next grade without missing a step, and with the rest of his class. In fact, and I would find this astounding about my dad had I not known him for so long, he actually went out for the high school baseball team that spring. He became their pitcher and had a pretty good year.

His father never took much to sports and never even knew my father played until one day an acquaintance said to him, "Hey, your boy is getting to be a pretty good ball player."

My grandfather came home and confronted my dad, asking if he was playing baseball. My dad replied yes, he was, and my grandfather asked if he was nuts. If he were to get hit or knocked down or whatever, it could spell disaster. My father replied he wasn't going to just sit around doing nothing, afraid to move because he might get hurt. He would play ball and that was all there was to it. You can't be afraid to live.

Life slowly began to return to what passed for normal with the Zonnevilles of Williamson.

The International Livestock Show was to be held in Chicago in the fall of 1941. My dad, his brother Duane, and several of his friends from farming families were, naturally, taking agriculture classes, and they thought it would be a grand idea to go to Chicago to the show.

Somehow, they convinced the Ag teacher and a local farmer, who'd only graduated a few years before, to drive. Two vehicles full of farm boys could easily drive across the country to visit the big city. He and his eight or ten buddies would pony up the cash for the trip. He and Duane had been raising chickens they could now sell to raise the cash. If they stayed in Milner Hotels—who only charged one dollar per night, so if you split that with another guy, that was fifty cents per night—and ate in diners, they could fill up on a dollar and a half per meal. Figuring two days up and two days back and a few days in Chicago, plus a little pocket money, why, they could do the whole trip for about fifty dollars each!

It would take them two days each way as, at the time, there were no such things as throughways or turnpikes. It was two-lane roads all the way, with low speeds and bumpy, sometimes unpaved roads to travel. But think of the adventure!

The trip went without a hitch. No accidents, no bumps, no bruises. A few young men snuck out in the middle of the night in Cleveland to attend a burlesque show, but no harm, no foul. Though I would've loved to have been witness to these rural farm boys as they took in their first burly Q show. Ah, the big city and all the sins laid out on a plate! They were taken on sightseeing tours while in Chicago, a city which soon became one of my father's favorite places to visit. While passing through Toledo, they even got to attend a show by the famous Nicholas Brothers, stars of the stage and the screen, and considered to be the finest tap dancers of their day. They were now world travelers! They chatted all the way back to Williamson how their stories would impress friends and girls throughout the county. Quite an adventure indeed!

It would appear as though 1941 was finally turning around and life would take on the simple routine of farming, working, studying, living, and growing.

Military Service Begins

December 7, 1941. Their world changed forever as they walked down Main Street in Williamson on the way to the soda shop for some ice cream, or maybe a phosphate. The Japanese, without provocation, bombed Pearl Harbor in Hawaii. People shouted the news as they walked along. No one could believe it. The United States could no longer avoid it: we were at war.

The United States declared war with Japan on December 8 and Germany declared war with the US on December 11. We were not just at war, we were hip-deep starting out.

As my father was now a senior in high school and would graduate come June, he was well aware he was about to be thrown into the war as well. The military would come calling and he would have to answer. His folks didn't want him to have anything to do with the war. They had left Holland to be away from forced service. They hadn't come three thousand miles for their son to be drafted. Plus, I would assume, there was a certain amount of trepidation at the possibility of losing a son they'd thought lost less than a year before when he'd been run over by a car. The choice would not be easy: family or country.

But we as a country had been attacked and my father was not one to stand on the sidelines. He wanted to go. He would fight for all this country had given his family and him. He graduated, at 17, in June of 1942. He would have to wait until January before he would be allowed by the powers that be to sign up for the draft. His parents would never sign off on him joining early.

When he did sign up, he told them he was ready to serve now! At the time there was a military exemption for farmers, as they had to grow the food needed for the war effort. He told them to forget the exemption—he wanted to serve. As the military was having trouble filling their quotas, they were only too happy to take him up on his offer. Very quickly he was signed, his hand was shaken, and he was now part of the United States effort to defeat the Nazis and Japs (as they were commonly called at the time).

Needless to say, his parents were not pleased with his decision. His mother was infuriated by his impulsive choice and refused to speak to him about it. She stated firmly she would not go to the train station to see him off. She would have no part of this. His father drove him to the station but did not wait for the train. He pulled up to the station, shook his son's hand, wished him luck, and drove off, leaving my dad to begin this new life standing on a train platform alone.

He was inducted into the United States Army at Fort Niagara, New York, and immediately shipped by train to Fort McClellan, Alabama. Due to the war effort, extra train cars were hard to come by. You needed so many to ship supplies, soldiers, armaments, and gear to the ports to be sent overseas. And those supplies required a massive amount of room, leaving the leftover, unneeded railcars for shipping human cargo. Recruits could be squeezed into railcars like sardines, and they were, packed in so tightly they slept in sitting or half-standing positions as the train roared through the night.

It took two very uncomfortable days and, almost, sleepless nights to reach Fort McClellan. It was near impossible to really sleep, seated in the cramped conditions or leaning against the rocking side of the railcar. Plus the excitement and anticipation of heading to boot camp had nerves on edge and stomachs flip-flopping. He told me that, like most seventeen-year-old boys, he really didn't know fear, couldn't imagine anything untoward happening to him. Hell, he'd been run over by a car and lived to tell about it, what could war bring? He was going to kick some Nazi ass, win the war and come home a hero. He was immortal. All seventeen- and eighteen-year-old boys are. That is why we send them to fight.

Once in, they were randomly assigned to platoons and housed in wooden barracks, each man setting up his new home on a cot with a wooden box at the end to store all their needs. It was not a big box. It didn't need to be, as they had only brought the clothes on their backs, and those clothes would soon be discarded for Army green. They soon realized they would have very few needs from here on out that the Army would not provide.

Showers, bathrooms, and any other personal needs you might have were in a different, community, building. Privacy was gone. The only thing private in the Army was your title and that was also your name. You had become just another nameless, faceless stranger amongst thousands of other nameless, faceless strangers. All brought together for one reason: to become soldiers who could fight, kill, or die, whatever would serve the ultimate purpose. You were to be a tiny cog in the war machine and your job was to help the U.S. military win this war for your country, no matter how you contributed.

They dropped what little they had brought from home onto the bare cot and were immediately ushered outside and, in a disorderly line, moved to another building for their shots. The army did not take chances you might bring more than a change of underwear from home. And they were making damn sure you were not going to pass whatever you might have brought along to the other occupants of the barracks. Then on to the quartermaster for bedding, uniforms, and rifles. Originally, they were issued Springfield rifles from World War I. A Springfield rifle would fire, and you could probably hit what you were aiming at, or at least get close to it, but they were not exactly state-of-the-art weapons. Before too long they were issued the new Garland M1 rifle, a far superior weapon.

The Garland M1 was a .30 caliber semiautomatic rifle that could fire forty to fifty rounds of ammunition per minute and had an effective firing range of five hundred yards. Very important when you had people shooting and running towards you with death in their eyes. The greater the range, the happier the shooter. If you missed at six hundred yards you could still squeeze off a few more rounds as the target increased in size while getting closer. They learned to shoot quickly.

Thus, began thirteen weeks of basic training. Not having been through basic, I had no idea what all that entailed. My father was happy to expound and educate.

"This was no eight-hour, five days a week job," he emphasized. "You weren't getting overtime after forty hours. We were up with the sun and had no idea what time it was when we were finally allowed to go to bed and were too tired to care. It was dark, you were exhausted, and you knew for a fact it would begin again far too early the next day. They were extremely long days and a lot of nights. Your drill Sergeant wanted to impress on you the fact that war was not a nine-to-five job, but a twenty-four-hour a day attempt to stay alive and keep those around you in the same condition.

"I really didn't mind," he continued, "as I played all kinds of sports in high school—plus working a farm isn't easy—so I was actually in pretty good shape. Still, no matter how good of shape you might think you're in, the Army thinks you can be better. And they are more than happy to test you over and over to prove it. Everyone has their limits. The Army was going to find them, push them, and expand them. When you are fighting for your life, you can't allow fatigue to lose what the military has spent so much time and energy investing in.

"You also had to learn to adjust to all kinds of new things, many of which you'd never dreamed of, including learning to eat things you'd never heard of before or seen. I had never eaten spaghetti, didn't know what it was or how to eat it. I made quite a mess of it until the guy across the table showed me how to roll it on the fork. But when the Army served you food, you didn't get to order from the menu. Whatever they slop on the tray is what goes into your stomach. If you're hungry enough you will eat anything, and sometimes that is the choice between life and death.

"Also, my father didn't like things like tomatoes and onions, so my mother never put them on the table. In our house my father was

God, and what he ate, we ate, and what he didn't like, we didn't need to know about. We ate a lot of Dutch fare: Dutch slaw (a kind of potato salad with vinegar, bacon and lettuce), scisizzone (a kind of dumpling filled with sausage and baked), Old World food. It's funny, really. We were not allowed to learn anything about the Old Country, they wouldn't speak of it, but my father couldn't quite give up the foods he loved from back there.

"Add that to the fact you are now sharing a bedroom with thirty-five other guys who snore and wheeze, breathe hard and cough, and sometimes weep for their mothers in the middle of the night when they think no one can hear them. It takes some getting used to. You feel like you're sleeping in the middle of Grand Central Station.

"And let me tell you, sharing a bathroom and showers with thirty-five strangers is no picnic. No matter how much you think you're used to sharing a single room or an outhouse with your brothers, as well as various wildlife, well, you learn to adjust your concept of normal. Normal is what the military tells you it is and that is all you need to know.

"All this comfort and convenience and you got paid fifty dollars a month, less the cost of the $10,000 life insurance policy the military demanded you acquire—to take of your loved ones in case you didn't listen closely enough to your drill Sergeant—and you actually pocketed a little over forty bucks a month. Not bad, really. You didn't have any expenses except what you blew in town or because you couldn't control your habits. Someone was always borrowing a few bucks here and a fiver just until payday. It helps keep a unit tight. When you see the guy that owes you thirty bucks is in trouble, you protect him. At least until the debt is paid.

"Training was rigorous, as they had a limited amount of time to get hundreds of thousands of men into shape and turned into soldiers, and not just a soldier, but a good soldier. Bad soldiers they didn't have to train, you arrived that way. If they just wanted bodies, the military could've saved billions by giving you a uniform and a gun and pointing you east. So, they pushed. A good soldier is an asset and a bad soldier can cost others their lives."

There was calisthenics, marching, of course, long hikes in full gear. These hikes would encompass just a few miles per day in the beginning of boot camp but quickly morphed into twenty-five to thirty miles a day. All while carrying forty-five pounds of gear in your rucksack. Then it was on to rifle training, learn your weapon better than you know your girlfriend. Spending a huge amount of time learning marksmanship on the range, as well as proper care and maintenance. Then there was the combat training. Can you change a clip while laying on your back in mud up past your face? And then more combat training, where they learned to fight with whatever was at hand: bayonets, hand to hand, teeth, feet, knees, or whatever might be laying on the ground close by. Your job as a soldier who belonged to the United States Army was to keep their property in good working order, and alive.

During all of this training, somehow the Army found the time to test these raw recruits to see what they might be best suited for to fulfill the Army's needs. They are called the ASTP's. the Army Specialized Training Program. That is efficiency.

My father was called in for his sounding and was informed that he had done very well on the tests and they believed he had a high IQ. Well, so much for Army testing! Obviously, the tests or the results were flawed! I kid because I love.

He was told that after basic, he would be sent on to the University of Alabama for further assessment. Once they had tested and assessed further he would be assigned to where they thought he would be the most useful to their needs. After just a couple days he was sent to Manhattan College in New York City to study engineering. Closer to home but further from where he wanted to be. He wanted to be on the battle lines, either in Europe or the Pacific, not sitting in a classroom in New York. But the Army does not care what you want, it cares about what it needs. Period!

But my father had the temperament of an eighteen-year-old and the pigheadedness of a Zonneville and he knew what was best for him. In a battle of wills between the Army and my father, I am glad I was not in the middle or, really, not born yet. That had to be a battle royal!

My father won. He just refused to do the work, refused to study, and the Army was left with no other choice but to grant him his wish. They shipped him off to Fort Bragg, North Carolina, and Airborne School.

Within two days they determined he had a bum knee—probably from either the car running him over, or from sports—and they sent him packing to Camp Forrest, Tennessee. He was to join the Eighth Infantry Division, 121st Infantry Regiment. The problem was they weren't there. They were out in the field on maneuvers.

When he found them and gave the first sergeant his orders, the sergeant looked him up and down and remarked, "We don't have any of y'all in this unit."

"Any of what?" my father asked, confused.

"Yankees," he deadpanned. "See, this here is a Southern unit."

"Well," my dad shrugs, "I'm about as Yankee as you can get. I'm from New York but I think we're all fighting the same people this time." The first sergeant agreed, and a truce was established.

According to my father's recollection, they were all very good soldiers and he prided himself on being the same, so he fit in. Plus as a farm boy from an obvious modest and rural background, they discovered they had much more in common than differences. He also learned when people take the time to discover what they share rather than what is dissimilar, you can get along with just about anybody.

While getting to know his new friends, my father found out that while he had been working his way through basic training and putting his full effort into failing out of engineering school, the unit he would soon join was working its ass off to become a hard fighting battalion. They had been training and working together, learning and becoming cohesive as a unit. Spending time in the middle of winter at Fort Leonard Wood, Missouri. It was bitter cold that winter and they fought frostbitten hands and feet while they continued their training.

As the Army likes its extremes, they then shipped out to train in the deserts of Arizona and California. Maybe the folks in charge decided if the units had no idea what the weather would be like where they were going, the chances of someone leaking that information was nil. So the regiment left Missouri in March of 1943 for the Desert Training Center in Yuma, Arizona.

Baking, now, in the sweltering heat with the sun beating on them, like a hammer on an anvil, it tested the best of them. Some wilted, some grew strong in the furnace. Those who were able to withstand the harsh ordeal headed back to Camp Forrest in August. That was where my father caught up to them out in field maneuvers. They were hardened, tough, and ready to be blooded. They had become closer than brothers by adversity and reliance on each other. He had found where he fit in. These were to be his present and future comrades in arms. He had found a home. He would have to prove it to them, but he was confident they would see his full mettle.

They continued preparations for overseas deployment for the next three months, and on November 25, they headed for Fort Dix, New Jersey, to be deployed to Europe. They hadn't been told where in Europe, but they knew they would soon be fighting the Nazis, and that was all they cared about.

To the best of his recollection they sailed December 5, 1943 aboard the S.S. Columbia, a former French liner, for "somewhere in the U.K."

The S.S. Columbia was a fine ship for a liner, and probably was quite comfortable for the three hundred or so she was designed to carry, but for the more than fifteen hundred men and gear clogged and jammed on her for this voyage, it was a bit tight. The men slept wherever they could make space, hanging hammocks, literally, from stem to stern, on every deck, fore and aft.

My Dad soon realized he was following basically the same route his father and grandparents had sailed to come to America, only in reverse. It was the same winter crossing with the same, he assumed, storm-crossed seas. It was bitterly cold with the waves crashing and spilling over the sides of the ship, swamping the deck with frigid seawater. Everything was coated with ice. The decks were slick as spit and twice as dangerous. A minute on deck was an hour of warming. On a good portion of the voyage the men were not allowed on deck as the seas were too rough; the powers that be didn't want any of the soldiers—they were hardly sailors—washing over the side.

They sailed in a convoy, as the German submarines were out patrolling the north Atlantic trying to sink as many ships as they could before they could deliver their cargo to the war. And if misery loves company, this was a very joyous cruise. Many of these young soldiers had never been on a calm lake, let alone a raging ocean, and seasickness ran rampant. My father's constitution was a bit sterner, or maybe he was just lucky; the constant motion did not affect him.

Normally a passage from New York to Ireland would take five days. Because of weather and routing, their voyage took fifteen days before they docked at Belfast, Northern Ireland. Though mid-winter, the men of the 121st almost danced off the S.S. Columbia. Yes, the land was cold. Yes, the land was thousands of miles from home. Yes, the land was foreign. But the land was *land*. Solid, firm, unmoving, and beneath their wobbly feet and legs. It was the most welcome thing they could think of. Well, a beer would've been nice.

Little did my father realize that it would be another twenty-one months before he would see his home again. He would live through two Thanksgivings, two Christmases, two birthdays, truly bitter cold, and the hell of war. Witnessing inhumanity on a scale he heretofore never could have imagined. An entire life condensed in those months. The eighteen-year-old boy was about to grow into a man more quickly than he could ever have envisioned.

Once they got their land legs back, they were transported to an estate the army had leased from British publisher Lord Beaverbrook in Northern Ireland. it was time for more intense preparation, for training that had the immediacy of war. It was time to get extremely serious about readying for a landing in Europe and facing a hardened, battle-tested Nazi army.

Winter in Northern Ireland is a series of cold, damp, short days and long, cold, damp nights. Breakfast and dinner were served in the dark, and lunch was served under overcast skies. They lived in Quonset buildings with a single heater in the middle which did little to warm or chase the damp from the room.

Training took on an intensity and ruggedness as they were pushed to their physical limits. All the hard work and preparation they put in now could save their lives later. Every man knew it and lived with that knowledge. Very few complained of the cold, the damp, or the hard work. They knew in their bones things were about to get much, much worse.

After a couple months of training, General Eisenhower issued an order that two men from the regiment were to be sent to the British Army near Belfast and they, in turn, would send two of theirs to the Americans. The two allies were doing this throughout their armies stationed across the British Isles. The idea was to improve relations and co-operation between the two allies; a two-week sharing of cultures.

In their usual wisdom the Army sent my Dad and sergeant Ruil Cot from L Company. Remembering it, Dad laughed as he said "It was quite an experience."

The British were a bit envious of the two Americans, as they discovered the pay scale in the American Army was quite a bit higher than the British, and their food was better than the Brits got as well. Of course, most of that was due to the fact the British had to share with the civilian population their limited resources. He couldn't believe how many items were rationed in Britain as opposed to home. It was a hard reminder that the British people had been at war far longer than the U.S. And they had endured almost constant bombing by the German air force for several years. They had blackouts every night. You had to respect the Brits and all they had sacrificed to hold on to their freedom and autonomy. Women, children and the elderly had given up so much just to survive and these men, these British soldiers, carried that with them in their hearts and on their shoulders. The strength of their character was astounding to dad. His respect for them was unlimited.

The folks back home, aside from a certain inconvenience of rationing, lived fairly normal lives. Well, except for the worry they carried every day in their hearts for loved ones now heading into war.

The people of Europe suffered massive devastation of cities, destruction of homes, businesses and infrastructure, as well as shortages of all necessities, especially food. Civilian casualties were high as well. There is no place to hide in the midst of a war.

All my father and his compatriots could do was prepare.

LANDING IN EUROPE

If there is one great misconception about World War Two, it is that D-Day was just that, one day. In point of fact, June 6, 1944 was just the beginning of a very hard-fought amphibious landing by the Americans, British, Canadian and Free French forces. It would take almost a week to completely secure the beach. The American forces had successfully established a beachhead on Omaha Beach within the first day, the deadliest, most horrifying, and hardest-fought day on the most heavily defended beach. Getting that foothold in the beach was costly and they sustained over two thousand casualties between 6:30 AM and the end of the day. One hundred and fifty-six thousand American troops stormed Omaha Beach that day.

D-Day was reminiscent of the oceans crossed to finally arrive at this point of the war. Wave after wave of men and machines crashing hard against the beach. Wading through the foaming sea, running, dodging fire, and bleeding. The dark, red blood flowed back into the sea. The oil from the vehicles, destroyed by shells and grenades, mixed with the blood of men, soaking into the sand and squishing red beneath the feet of the next wave of infantrymen. The roar of cannon and rifle fire, machine guns spitting in a deathly staccato. The Germans, dug in for months, threw everything they had at man and machine storming the beaches. The sound and fury of hand-to-hand, up close, battle. The screams and cries of the wounded woven in with the shouts of orders, prayers, and curses, mixing with exploding shells hurtling from the ships a quarter-mile out to sea. Demolition teams pushing explosives under the wood and iron barricades that appeared as though they had grown there like a thick forest, breaking their way through barbed wire stretched like razors across the sand. The waves crashing on the beach had been drowned by the noise of men killing other men, so their fellows might live and find purchase on the beach.

Others would crawl over the top of the dead and dying, moving inch by inch, life by life into the jaws of the German fire.

It took until June 11 to fully secure all the beaches. My father landed on June 10, 1944. They jumped into shoulder-deep water to make their way to the beaches. By then the fighting was almost non-existent compared to what others had faced only days before. He believes more men died due to drowning, as they were carrying sixty to eighty pounds of gear in full dress, while attempting to wade to shore, than were actually killed by the Germans that day. He mentioned the scent of death was heavy as they landed. The sand reeked of blood and gunpowder and it looked as though the end of the world had come. You could hear the war off in the distance, but the beach was silent as if a sacred place, a haunted site where you felt the ghosts thick as tree limbs around you. Not a place where you wanted to stop and reflect. It was piece of land to be gotten through as quickly as possible.

It had been early June when the 121st was ordered to pack up and ready themselves for the invasion of Europe. They were transported to Belfast and loaded on to Liberty ships. Nicknamed "Ugly Ducklings," Liberty ships were cargo vessels designed for emergency use during the war. They were built to standardized, mass production designs, with parts shipped from all over the country to a central locale, from whence they could be assembled as quickly as four and a half days. These utilitarian vessels would transport men and supplies to Normandy. They weren't pretty, hence the name, but they served their purpose well.

As they closed in on the beach the men were transferred to landing craft that would transport them as close to the beaches as possible. The men would drop over the side of the ships and climb down cargo nets, dozens at a time, to quickly fill the transports. A number of men never got past the transfer, getting hung up in the ropes, breaking arms and legs or dropping into the roiling sea. The transports would drop them off in the surf before heading back to the Ugly Ducklings for more men and supplies.

They assembled at the staging areas up from the beach and closer to where the front was now located. It was time to join the fight. My father was to remain with Lt. William Reed to scout the area nearby and then move forward toward the waiting Germans. My father respected Lt. Reed as much as any man or officer he'd ever met. He was just a good officer and a better man who was soon to become company commander. A position he wouldn't, unfortunately, hold for long, as he was wounded just outside Saint-*Lô* in northwestern France. The company commander made it approximately thirty-five miles inside France before he was sent home. His war was over.

My dad and his battalion began their fight in the hedgerows in and around Normandy. These are just what they sound like: rows of hedges, trees, and shrubs that had occupied this territory for hundreds of years, marking boundary lines of ownership. They had grown so closely together and their roots so intermingled that even tanks could not penetrate this living wall. Of course, they only had one opening from field to field, so they were incredibly easy to defend. And almost impossible to attack and take. You funneled men through this tiny opening and into fire.

The casualties were high and climbing as they fought across this open farmland with little or no cover, especially when the only way to get from one piece of land to the next was to funnel through these tiny openings. This was where my dad received his first Purple Heart. His wounds inflicted by hand grenade were not serious—certainly not serious enough to get him out of the fight—but serious enough to require some medical attention. That was the medic's job. Medics were partially trained medical assistants who would use every piece of knowledge glommed from every other medic to patch up soldiers, hit them with morphine, and get them back on their feet, or at least away from the front where they could get proper medical attention. These were some of the many unsung heroes of war, performing near-miracles with little or no supplies and not enough training. They saved more lives through pure force of will than many of the doctors did with proper facilities.

Dad had been hit but he had no desire to leave the front. Besides, there were no good medical facilities nearby, and they were short on men due to heavy casualties. So unless you simply couldn't do it, you were expected to continue on with your unit, which my father was only too happy to do. These were his friends and some of the finest people he knew, he had no desire to leave them.

His sergeant, though, who had been a bit of bastard and a bully back in Northern Ireland, gifted himself a wound so he would be sent home. Apparently, the great bully was not as tough as he imagined and couldn't take the horror and terror of battle. Bullies seldom can.

They made my Dad sergeant, and they continued onward toward La Haye-du-Puits, Dinard, and then on to Brest. During these several weeks of fighting my Dad received his second Purple Heart incurred by artillery fire. Again, they were mostly lacerations of the arm, chest, leg, and stomach. He was beginning to wonder if his time wasn't near, as this was his second wounding sustained in a relatively short period of time.

But as he lay, waiting medical attention at the Army hospital—which is to say, tents just a ways back from the front lines—seeing the men awaiting surgeries and amputations, well, when he compared his total injuries to the injuries of these men, they didn't amount to much. He found himself embarrassed even to be in the same room with some of these men who had suffered much worse wounds. After a few days in the hospital he was gratefully returned to the front.

It is hard to complain about shrapnel wounds easily repaired while sitting next to someone who has lost an arm or a leg or, God forbid, half their face. War is truly horrifying when seen up close and in person.

"At a ceremony held upon a battlefield of this campaign and upon ground conquered by this regiment, I had the pleasure of awarding the Certificate of Merit to your son, Sergeant Robert E. Zonneville." So began the letter my grandmother received, dated February 27, 1945. It stated that Sergeant Zonneville (Private Zonneville at the time), coming across a scattered group of disorganized men, got them reorganized, and helped repulse a German attack. Hence the Sergeant in front of his name. Not long after, they wanted to promote him to lieutenant, but he knew the Germans were targeting officers, so he declined the offer.

Once out of the care of the medical staff, he returned to his squad. There is something in the solidarity of a company of men at war that brings them together, closer than family, closer than friends from childhood. Living with death, watching fellows fall or be horribly wounded, brings men together in a way like none other. Soldiers share something deep in the soul the rest of us can only envy. So it was with great joy he returned to the front. That may be the only time you will ever read those words put together like that.

It would seem his squad now spent most of their time crisscrossing France. People always think of a war as just that, the war. A great undertaking encompassing time and territory. But wars are hundreds of small battles, taking town after town, sometimes block after block, to advance your position. Everyone remembers the grand battles of a war, but the soldiers remember the towns, the streets, the muddy lanes.

After landing at Omaha Beach, doing recon and preparing to engage the enemy on the front, they spent the next month, basically from July 4 through August 5, making their way to La Haye-du-Puits and Saint-*Lô,* where he had suffered his second wounding. From August 6 through August 15 they fought their way back east, taking Dinard. Their division then returned to the Atlantic coast, joining other companies fighting to complete the liberation of Brest, from August 20 through September 11, and finally securing the Crozon Peninsula between September 13 and September 18. The combat was brutal as they weeded out the remaining German troops, who'd had plenty of time to dig in defensive positions and to set booby traps filled with explosives and shrapnel. The casualties were high on the American side before subduing and securing the area. Their reward was a couple days R and R before being shipped out to Luxemburg.

Their time in Luxemburg was primarily a defensive position, so it allowed them a bit of a rest and some time to heal their wounds. They could catch their collective breath without the worry of constant battle as they defended Medernach, Diekirch, Gilsdorf, Reisdorf and Beaufort.

Too often we all forget, or really just have no idea, that front line infantry troops suffer tremendous losses. Not all of those wounds are visible to the naked eye. It is not just death they face every day: that is a given; hell, sometimes that is a blessing. No, it is the incapacitating wounds, loss of limbs, head trauma, burnt flesh and minds, which cause tremendous physical pain and deep psychological anguish. The conditions they are forced to endure, by virtue of the circumstances, are horrific and terrible. They are at the mercy of rain, snow, wind, and sleet, with slick mud sucking at each step. The clammy, damp cold that buries itself deep in your bones, threatening never to leave. And then it is the heat and humidity, in the midst of summer, sapping their strength until they wilt like dying flowers. It is a constant battle, not just with the enemy, but with the elements as well. And when you are not fighting for your life and sanity, advancing through this hell, you are digging a foxhole, as deeply into the ground as an entrenching tool can make possible, to provide what little protection Earth and hope can afford from the artillery shells dropping on top of you and the shrapnel flying in every direction.

The meals they were issued were K rations, each meal the size of a Cracker Jack box sealed in wax to keep the elements at bay. Breakfast was comprised of a small can of eggs, hard biscuits, and instant coffee. The mid-day meal was a small tin of cheese, hard biscuits, and a lemon powder, so they could attempt to conjure some kind of drink and pretend it was lemonade. And for dinner there was a small can of pork, hard biscuits, and bouillon. If they could get down low enough in the foxhole and out of sight they could heat hot water in their canteen cup by burning the wax-coated box, and thus make coffee or bullion. It was food, and it sustained, but that was about all. I don't believe I ever saw my Dad eat another hard biscuit in my life.

The infantry, I was to learn, has very few comforts and a high rate of casualties. Hell, even going to the bathroom on the front presented all kinds of challenges. You think finding a bathroom on the highway can be difficult? Try finding one on a battlefield.

As the late war journalist Ernie Pyle once wrote, "At times the conditions these men live in are almost as bad as the fighting." At least periodically the Army would rotate them back, away from the front lines, so they could shower, get clean clothes, and enjoy a hot meal. Little things mean a lot.

After far too short of a time in their defensive position in Luxembourg, the 121st was sent to the *Hürtgen* Forest, one hundred and seven miles from their current position, along with the rest of the 8th Division.

Their mission was to relieve a division that had been on the front line too long. The battle of the *Hürtgen* had begun in mid-September and it was now mid-November. They needed relief, and now! So the army decided that rather than have my dad's division walk the entire one hundred and seven miles, their normal mode of getting from point A to all points in between, they would truck them the first seventy or so miles, and they could stretch their legs the last thirty-some miles. The soldiers really didn't mind as they, at least, were getting a ride most of the way. Though slogging across more than thirty miles of rain-soaked mud, in cold, damp temperatures, through a cloud-locked day and a sleet and rain-filled night would be no picnic.

I would venture to say most people have never heard of the battle of the *Hürtgen* Forest. I wouldn't know of it except my dad fought there. A little WWII history:

The Battle for the Huertgen Forest was a series of brutal engagements between the American and German forces which took place between mid-September and December 16, 1944. The forest lay just east of the Belgium-Germany border. It was the longest battle fought on German land, and, also, the longest single battle the United States has ever fought.

The American forces were trying to pin down the Germans, so they couldn't send reinforcements to their front lines up the Siegfried Line. This was a line of twenty-two thousand fortifications of pill boxes and bunkers, tank traps, and mine fields. The line of defense ran along their western border with France and was referred to as the West Wall. It had been built in secret over three years between 1936 and 1939. It was then abandoned in 1940 as unnecessary, as the Germans poured across their border into France. In 1944, as the Allies fought their way onto the beaches of Normandy and then on across France, the Siegfried Line was rearmed and three hundred and sixty thousand people were put to work to re-dig and rebuild the defenses. It was one of the most defended and most difficult pieces of land to take.

The Germans wanted to stymie the American push forward and to inflict as many casualties as they could, hoping to stop the American assault. The Battle for the Huertgen Forest would cost the U.S. First Army 33,000 casualties, total dead and wounded.

The Germans did not want to surrender one inch of this land, as they were using it as a staging area for the Battle of The Bulge. It was also an asset as a perfect location for commanding and protecting access to the mountains around the *Ruhr Valley Dam.* Therefore this became one of the hardest-fought and costliest battles of the war, even though today it is largely forgotten, as it led directly into the more well-known Battle of the Bulge.

History in a nutshell complete. If you would like to know more about this battle, there are many references on the Web and in these things they call *books*.

My father's division arrived in the middle of the cold, sleet- and snow-filled night to where he would describe as Hell with icicles. The Huertgen had everything one would need to make a continued existence almost impossible: rain, snow, thick forest, mines, pillboxes, heavy artillery, trench foot and frozen toes. They would see legs, arms, and other body parts scattered where they had been blown off by mines, left where they'd fallen, as there was neither time nor manpower to properly dispose of them, creating a nightmarish abyss of hope. It was just a brutal, horrible situation. The cold seeped and burrowed into their bones, the sleet cold and constant, and the oppressive skies pushed hard on their spirits. They could never seem to find any warmth. Just cold. They would have given anything for a warm blanket, a decent pair of gloves, or a pair of dry socks. A simple hot cup of coffee would have felt like the greatest of God's gifts. Just a simple cup of hot *anything* would have been the ultimate treat.

The Germans held all the advantages. A defense built over years and, though abandoned for a while, had been rebuilt and reinforced, with men and machines dug deeply into the forest around them. The forest was thick with evergreen trees and had few roads or tracks. The Allied superiority in air power was defeated by the lack of visibility and thick forest. The Germans had had plenty of time to sight in the few roads with their mortars and artillery.

Though the Americans held a great advantage in numbers, a five-to-one advantage by most accounts, it was nullified by the terrain and conditions. They were just providing more targets for the Germans machine gunners. A couple divisions had held the ground before the 8th showed up. They had spent the last month or more chewing up what Germans they could find, and trying not to be chewed up by the ones hiding in amongst the trees and bunkers. The Americans also were to learn of a cute little thing called "tree bursts." The Germans had discovered that if they timed the explosion of artillery just right, they could make it explode at treetop level, thereby sending blazing, hot shrapnel and wood splinters in all directions, especially towards the ground. American soldiers had been trained to hit the deck when they heard artillery shells coming, so this tactic, combined with the Americans' training, increased deaths and casualties. This is what they walked into on November 20th. They would spend the next month fighting for inches and praying for salvation. The Germans, though many were just boys and inexperienced, made the American soldiers pay dearly for every scrap of land they gained. As I mentioned, the cost in human lives, suffering, and munitions was staggering.

After almost a month of hard-fought battles and slow, agonizing movement of troops and material, they reached the town of Obermaubach, which lay east of the town of Huertgen on the Rur River. They rolled and staggered into the town on Christmas Day 1944. It had been the evening previous, while sitting in a foxhole after surviving hell for the last month, that my father had penned his letter home.

They crossed the Rur and secured the city of Duren soon after, erecting a sign which read "Entering Duren, courtesy of the 8th infantry division." It was time to hunker down once again. They would hold this position for almost a month while the Allied forces consolidated their military strength to make a last effort to defeat, once and for all, the Nazi forces. And though Duren was cold and wet, it was still a welcome respite from the previous month. Sometimes the smallest gifts are the most treasured, and a month holding a defensive position was a gift from the constant fighting of the front. They would soon join forces with the rest of the Army fighting the Battle of The Bulge for a final push to break the back of the German forces.

They left Obermaubach in early February, fighting their way to the Rhine, then on to meet up with Russian divisions near Schwerin, Germany. From February 24th through March 30th they pushed their way through Wenau, Gurzenich, Duren, east of the Rur River, Girbelsrath, Blatzheim, Kerpen, Mödrath, Froehen, Gleuel, Hürth, Hermülheim, Bonn and Lengerich. Battles not well known, but fought nonetheless. Then from March 30th through April 15th they fought through another seventeen towns and battles, finally making their way to the Elbe river, finishing off battles in Münster, Bleckede, Hinterhagen, Gülze and, finally, Schwerin by V-E day. April 27, 1945: a joyous day for the Allied troops in Europe.

Along the way the 8th division took in 244,600 prisoners, including more than 55,000 in one day as they arrived in the capital of Mecklenburg. The German soldiers, being most observant and closer to reality than their superiors, could see the writing on every wall along the way. So after a while, they just began surrendering to the division as the 8th Infantry made their way towards Schwerin. I am told the 8th were the first foreign troops to set foot in this area since Napoleon's troops conquered Mecklenburg in 1806.

It was now early May and the war was over. They were spending most of their time taking in prisoners, dealing with thousands of half-starved, filthy, slave laborers hoping for salvation courtesy of the American troops. The rest of their time was spent searching out enemy soldiers still hiding, holding out against the hope the Third Reich would find a way to rise again. Apparently, they believed they could still defeat the oncoming Americans by attacking the flanks of the advancing troops, This belief did not serve the enemy soldiers well. All were killed or taken prisoner. The 8th also spent a good amount of time manning the POW, refugee, and displaced person camps.

And more importantly still, the population of the area had grown by a magnitude of seven and it was up to the Americans to find necessities for all. They had to come up with food, clothing, and shelter for the civilians now pouring into the secured area, as well as for the POW's. And they still had to meet up with the Russians coming through from the eastern front and, then, coordinating with them on the cleaning up portion of war.

During this time of coordination and governing they discovered and liberated two Nazi concentration camps near *Wöbbelin*; one for women and children, and the other just for men. Many of the prisoners, obviously, were Jews and Gypsies, but there were also people brought in from Poland, Russia, Greece, France, Italy, Czechoslovakia, Holland, and Germany.

As is pointed out in the history of the 121st Regiment: "War, in spite of its horrors and destruction, had rules. All of them had been broken by the enemy . . . "

They found more than twenty-five hundred weak, starving beings, hardly recognizable as humans. It was a horrific, despicable sight that left these men, these soldiers, who had just spent ten months of hard, bloody, hell battling their way across a destroyed Europe, sick to their stomachs and, even more, sickened in their souls.

The male prisoners had been more harshly oppressed and tortured. The liberating forces discovered a common burial plot with 381 bodies thrown in and open pits with two hundred more nearby.

My father never told us any of this until recently. He described it this way: "The sights and smells were terrible. These were stick figures of skin and bone who weighed next to nothing. How could any human being treat people like this? If I had seen a Nazi soldier at that time I would have killed him with my bare hands." I should mention my father was one of the kindest men I have ever known and would never, knowingly harm another, so this was quite a statement.

It was truly the most disgusting thing he, and any of his comrades, had ever had the horror to witness. Cells were stacked with what had once been people, now just masses of decaying humanity.

The people from the surrounding towns swore they had no idea this was taking place. My father said from the smell alone there could be no way they could NOT have known. You could smell the death from a thousand yards away.

They came across a nine-year-old Italian boy who had been sent to the camp after a Nazi officer had abused him and the boy had shot the officer. The boy was now an orphan and alone in the world, so some of the 8th smuggled him out of the camp. No one seemed to have a plan, just an action.

The military establishment of the 8th brought along the police commissioner from Schwerin who swore he knew nothing of all this. A young German Jew was chosen to explain to this fine man every single one of the abuses and atrocities committed by the Germans at the camp, while this upstanding citizen stood there, forced to listen. He could neither turn away nor walk away from this young man as he was quite aware of the glowering and extremely angry American soldiers with death in their eyes surrounding him. He should've considered himself lucky to be allowed to walk out of the camp.

Villagers from all the surrounding towns were brought to the camps, from *Wöbbelin*, Ludwigslust, Hagenow and Schwerin. Under the supervision of the Eighth Infantry Division, they were required to remove the bodies, including those in the pits, and to dig a proper grave for each person and to bury them, with respect, in their own town cemeteries. They were also ordered to erect either a Christian cross or a Star of David over each grave. Army chaplains of Catholic, Protestant, and Jewish faiths conducted the ceremonies.

Along with the religious marker was a stone on each grave with the inscription:

"Here lie the bodies of victims of Nazi atrocity from Poland, Russia, Greece, Czechoslovakia, France, Italy, Holland and Germany who died of starvation and brutality in the *Wöbbelin* concentration camp. Buried under the supervision of the 8th Infantry Division, U.S. Army, by whom the surviving prisoners of the camp were liberated. 'God is our refuge and our strength.'"

The war in Europe ended shortly thereafter.

I felt it necessary to include this op-ed piece by Paul Boesch, a friend of my father's. They had served together in the same company before the *Hürtgen* Forest campaign. Paul had been a platoon commander who had gotten promoted along the way until he became the commander of Company G. They became friends partially because they were some of the few who had landed together and were still around. When Paul wrote a book on the campaign, he used my dad as a reference, as Paul had been wounded and sent back, and my dad had served through the rest of the war. They remained friends throughout their lives.

This is one of the most amazing and heartfelt pieces I have read on the subject of going back and remembering. Not just remembering what happened to you, but taking the time to remember those who did not return. I hope his spirit doesn't mind my using this here. He has passed and so has the *Houston Post*.

Editorial by Paul Boesch

The Houston Post, November 28, 1985

Three years ago I tried to assuage a gnawing, disturbing memory by returning to battlefields I had known in World War II. The pilgrimage failed when I failed to orient myself. The Hürtgen Forest had known many years of prolific rebirth since I had crawled among its burned, broken and scarred trees in November 1944.

Yet something inside me just had to go back. Again. The visit in 1982 did not exorcise the ghosts I had thought to lose by returning to where so many had died in that exercise in bloody futility known as the Battle of the Huertgen Forest. Indeed, it only exacerbated the painful memory.

In the summer of 1985 I decided to try again, but this time I was better prepared. In the interim I had corresponded with three former German soldiers. Dr. Adolph Hohenstein, who had written a definitive history of the entire Huertgen Forest battle from the German viewpoint. He had used my book Road to Huertgen *as one of his sources. Klaus Schultz, who had made the battle his hobby, and Koni Schall, who has created a museum dedicated to the battle. These three promised, and provided, their help.*

Armed with current maps, some military charts of '44 and official permission from the forest authorities, we moved slowly form area to area. My mind wrestled with a thousand thoughts but refused to accept what it saw as authentic. The logging truck had changed portions of the forest completely. Fall colors gave an aura of beauty that disguised the fact the in '44 artillery and mortar shells had fallen at a rate estimated at 3,500 a day.

Demolitions experts have been at work since the end of the war trying to disarm the explosives. Yet, just two weeks before, two young boys had been killed when they found an unexploded mine and played with it.

Our road made a sudden right turn and started to cross a small stone bridge. My mind leapt to attention!

"Wait! Stop!" I shouted, "I remember this bridge!"

I clambered out of the car, and as I turned full circle, was surrounded by memories. This was the very spot where I had set up our first positions. I was a first lieutenant, the weapons platoon leader for

Company E. It was at this point that I had been ordered by Capt. William McKenna to set up machine guns. I was to use my mortar men as riflemen to protect the bridge that spanned the Weisser Weh Creek.

Yet, I wanted, and needed, more than the bridge to feed my voracious memory. I crossed the small creek and could not hold back the torrent of words as I told my guides how deep the mud had been around the bridge approach when we first arrived there. The combat engineers we detailed to fill the slimy area to facilitate the movement of tanks that were expected to arrive soon. In a steady stream, trucks came down the road, crossed the bridge, turned around and then dumped their load on the way out.

In spite of their many trips, suddenly, WHAM! One of the trucks struck an anti-tank mine. Men and pieces of truck flew everywhere. Quickly we gave all the help we could and dispatched the injured to the rear. Yet, the next morning I found one man whose life had ended in two feet of viscous mud.

Using that memory as a guide I walked slowly up the road, scanning the landscaped side of the hill. Then, I stopped and pointed: "Up there. Right up there we had a gun position: there should be a foxhole up there."

Schall looked at me incredulously. Then he turned and ran down the road about 25 yards and turned into the woods. Suddenly he appeared above us, but no foxhole.

"Go back ten or fifteen feet," I told him.

He did and within seconds there was a whooping and yelling!

"It is here," he screamed in German, "It is here!"

Now it was my turn to run, and I did. In a matter of moments I had joined him and saw the unmistakable outline of the hole I had helped dig 41 years before. It was about two feet wide, six feet long and a foot and a half deep. When we had dug it, it was more than three feet deep, but time and nature had slowly filled it with dust and dirt and leaves and branches.

A powerful emotion gripped me as I stood in it. To some it may have looked like a hole in the ground. To me it was a hole into history. A hole that was 41 years deep. Here I had slept, eaten, prayed and cowered. And longed for home and peace.

I was full of the heady, goose-pimple feeling of having discovered something, yet I was aware that there was more to be found. Things happen swiftly and often irrevocably in infantry combat. I became the executive officer of E Company when several officers became casualties. I remembered that I had moved to the other side of the Weisser Weh Creek, across the stone bridge, and established the "rear" command post (CP) less than a hundred yards from the one in which I stood.

Using the same scanning method, I quietly moved up the road, surveying every inch of a ledge that capped the sloping road bed. It was about 10 feet above us. Suddenly, I saw a change. There was a spot where the edge rose sharply about six inches. "Of course, I remember that we used the dirt we had dug out of the hole to gain additional protection from the foxhole."

"Up there, right up there!" I shouted, and Koni scrambled up the embankment. And there it was! The CP I had occupied during the worst day and night of my life. Thanksgiving Day, 1944.

I recalled for my friends how we had blindly obeyed an order that "every man was to have Thanksgiving dinner" and sent a carrying party up the hill. Artillery shells killed three men and wounded eight. The cans were never opened.

The path we all used to get up the hill was nearby, and Schall and I got down on our bellies to look for it. Still barren and bare, the path was visible when he looked under lush shrubs. I was full of memories of how many broken and bloody men we had carried down that path.

As we rose to our feet Schall bent down again and picked something out of the dirt. He looked at it and then placed it in my hand. The object was the projectile from a .30-caliber bullet. I stared at it, wondering how close it had come to me 41 years before.

Thanksgiving, 1944. All through the night a burning tank lit the area and rocked it with explosions. In my foxhole I nursed a captain whose nerves were shot. I made frequent morale trips through his company, which was lined up on the road where we now stood. German artillery, confused by the noise in our area, concentrated some of their most punishing barrages on the stone bridge area. Medics came frequently and did not leave empty-handed.

All these memories poured out of my mind, my heart, and my mouth. Then, I wanted quiet. I wanted to be alone. I walked up the road by myself, just as I had walked when I was ordered to take command of G Company and prepare to attack the town of Huertgen.

The emotional strain of so many memories brought a lump to my throat and tears from my heart. I remembered my reason for returning to the forest; the ghosts who had once been buddies and friends. I spoke to them. Yes, unashamedly I admit that I spoke to them aloud. I called them by name.

I wanted them to know they were not forgotten. That they will never be forgotten. Perhaps now they can sleep in tranquility, knowing that while even one of us is alive, their memory is preserved.

Homecoming

I am certain there are many stories left out of my father's time in Europe during the war. You cannot be on the front lines for most of eleven months and not have stories. Some he just didn't care to relive, some were a bit bawdy, not front line but R and R, and some he felt were just for him and those he served with. But after many discussions we came to the conclusion, his time of war was a defining moment in his life, but it did not define his life. So, I apologize if some of this seems a bit sketchy. There are thousands of well-written and brilliant books about the war. I suggest you read several to fully understand what these ordinary people accomplished.

They were soon advised that, after getting the area secured and order restored, they would be relieved by another division. After which they would be returned to the United States for thirty days R and R. They would then receive additional training and readied for deployment to the Pacific. Apparently the muckamucks in Washington wanted experienced troops to invade Japan. As my father states, the troops were not exactly overjoyed at this turn of events. They had suffered heavy casualties and extreme hardships over the last ten months and felt they had done their duty. But when the army calls you answer.

So, they packed up and headed toward La Havre, France for

transport back to the USA. They left on the USS General Bliss bound for Boston. The return trip would be far more relaxed as they were heading back to the USA victorious in their war with Nazi Germany. They would be afforded a little time to see friends and family before once again heading directly toward battle. And they would not be being chased by German U-boats intent on sending them to the bottom of the sea. That, alone, takes much of the tension out of the voyage.

They were headed home, if only for a short time, and the accommodations of the General Bliss were far less crowded and more much comfortable than on the Columbia and the trip would take less time. Whereas the Columbia had taken fifteen days in cold, hard seas the Bliss made the trip home in five.

Though, they ran into a small problem when it came time to disembark from the ship. Apparently, the nine-year old kid they had smuggled out of the concentration camp had now been smuggled, in a duffle bag, onto the ship. No one involved really had much of an idea of what they planned to do with the child once in America, all they knew is they were not leaving him in the hands of the military in Germany. The problem was you didn't know whose military was going to take control of what part of Germany. The U.S. was occupying some, the Russians were trying to occupy the world and the allies were stuck in the middle. All the soldiers knew was that this kid was not going to wind up in the hands of the Russians and they'd figure out the details the same way they'd won the war; one day, one town at a time.

When the ship docked the immigration officials in Boston, naturally, found the child and were not going to let the child off the ship and into America. He had no papers, no family, no one to claim him or raise him. They couldn't just let an unsupervised child loose in the country. Well, you really shouldn't go up against a group of men who had just beaten back the Nazi's. All agreed they would not leave the ship unless the boy was also allowed off and welcomed into the country. Checkmate.

Higher customs official summoned, wall of angry G.I's, boy allowed in, in the care of said customs official. Simple. They never knew what happened to the boy. He was allowed to stay and, my dad believes, the customs official was the one who adopted him.

The division disembarked and was taken to Camp Myles Standish for a big steak dinner and a chance for them to call home. Phones can be impersonal unless it is a loved one whom you have worried yourself sick over for the last two years. That phone call, that sound of a voice, is like holding each other in your arms. Families could be reassured by the sound of their son's voice that they were, indeed, home and safe; if only for a short period of time.

The very next day they were sent to Fort Dix, New Jersey where they were issued new uniforms, back pay and their golden ticket. Each was given a rail ticket home. The phone call had been wonderful, to hear each other's voices on the ends of the line, it was contact but not what all wished. Now, they would actually see, touch and hold each other. Though not a long trip for my father it would seem to take forever to get home.

His parents, now filled with pride at their returning decorated war hero, both came to pick him up at the railroad station in Rochester, New York on July17, 1945. A quick reunion, my grandparents, and the Dutch in general, not known for their outward displays of affection, and then the drive to Williamson.

My father recalled the trip as one of reflection. Here he was, a young man gone for the past two and a half years, twice wounded, recipient of Purple Hearts and several other medals and promotions. He had fought in a war in far off Europe and been victorious against the Nazi invaders, and he was still not old enough to vote nor buy a beer. It would be another six months before he reached the age of majority at that time in America of twenty-one.

Yes, here was a twenty-year-old, just home from the war, safely sitting in his dad's car, yet he couldn't shake one very real feeling, one very real fear. His division had suffered over a one hundred percent casualty rate. That means every man in this division had been wounded at least once and many had died. More than one hundred percent casualty rate! Many of the men he had trained with, fought with, served with would not be receiving the home coming he would enjoy. Others would be coming home but were severely wounded and would carry those wounds for the rest of their lives. He had been wounded twice, though neither had left him disabled. Now they were going to let him enjoy home for a month and then send him on to the Pacific, where he was expected to storm the beaches of Japan.

Was it possible he had used up all his luck and his number would come up over there? He, of course, never mentioned this to his parents-there being no need for unnecessary worry on their part-but he had to wonder if this would be the last time he would get to share with them. If this would be his last time to see his home and the town of his youth. As a result of these dark thoughts there was only one thing to do; he would live as if these were his last thirty-three days on this earth. He would live every day as if it were his last.

Grandma and Grandpa Zonneville had not been happy, had actually been extremely upset, when my father had enlisted in the Army. His mother not bothering to come to the railroad station. His father giving him a handshake and well wishes not bothering to get out of the car. But now he was returning from the war a decorated veteran, written up in the local papers and a bit of a celebrity. The local paper had also written a very nice article about him on his return to his home town; listing his battles and medals, his promotions and some of his exploits. Now pride swelled in the parental chests and his mother asked him to show up at her workplace so she could show off her famous son.

He spent a few days meeting her friends and fellow employees, the extended family had a large picnic to greet the returning war hero. By his own admission it was a bit overwhelming but a great deal of fun basking in the warm glow of admiration and familial love. He could take the time to enjoy the attention, especially when there were so many who would not share in this homecoming, and they were never far from his mind. But he decided that since they could not celebrate he would celebrate for all those who served and would not be returning to the land of their birth.

He allowed himself free reign to enjoy life. He drank too much and lived too hard, but he was going to enjoy some of life; especially after living like an animal for the past ten months. One can only imagine what it was like to trudge through rain, mud, snow, bitter cold, blood-soaked ground and death before returning to the states and having life laid out like a banquet before him. A few months earlier he was freezing in a foxhole, eating cold, hard biscuits and wondering if he had to take a dump whether it would cost him his life. Now this!

Quickly, around the second or third night home, he borrowed the family car to go out with friends for an evening of libations and merriment. After a night of drinking and carousing with old friends and new and now driving on roads he was no longer acquainted with he had a bad accident. The car was wrecked but by some quirk of fate neither he nor the two other fellas, nor the two girls with them, were badly injured, just a few bumps and bruises. However, getting his father out of bed at 2:30 AM was quite another story. Sometimes one wishes for more severe injuries to oneself so as to temper the retribution from the parents. His father was not happy with his war hero son. This was going to cost some cash and trust, neither of which he was flush in.

Near the end of the furlough as my father was, at least, mentally preparing himself once again for war-storming beaches and whatever the future would or would not hold-they dropped the first Atomic bomb on Hiroshima. A frightened hush fell with it all over the world. Three days later another fell upon the city of Nagasaki. On August 15th Emperor Hirohito announced the unconditional surrender of Japan. The war in the Pacific came to an end. My father would not be storming the beaches of Japan or anywhere else.

The military had established a point system for discharge from service and he was an excellent candidate for discharge. He had served twenty-one months in Europe, had a combat infantryman's badge, two Purple Hearts, a Bronze Star, a European Theater of Operations Medal with four bronze stars for serving in all four European campaigns, Occupation Medal, Victory Medal and a Good Conduct Medal. His regiment would later receive a Unit Citation for their action in the Huertgen forest. Add that to the Certificate of Merit and a medal from the State of New York for all accomplishments in service of country and it was an impressive stack!

My father reported back to Fort Leonard Wood in Missouri where he was assigned to help with training new recruits for a short period of time and giving them the benefit of his experience and knowledge and was finally discharged on October 12, 1945. He was still three months shy of his twenty first birthday.

A Civilian Once Again

Military service now officially behind him, my father returned home, not short term but for the long haul, to Williamson; as a civilian for the first time in a lifetime. His first official act as a civilian was to purchase a 1939 Ford in which to go off in search of a job. Though he readily admits he was nowhere near to being ready to settle down.

He was twenty, just released from war and deprivation, from witnessing the worst humanity could throw at him and he needed to decompress into 'normal'. We never stop to think of the impossibility when we ask those who have served this country in times of war to just put all that they have seen and experienced, all the horror they have lived, and maybe had to do to survive, behind them, and slip right back in to the bucolic American dream. We ask too much. Why we don't have a way to ease folks back into civilian life, to find a way to give them a chance to succeed, to allow them time and opportunity to decompress after witnessing the worst mankind can bring, well, that is for another book. This is for my father.

So, he decompressed on his own program. He had gotten a taste of how to adjust from military protocol to civilian freedom for a month earlier. Now it was time to jump in the deep end. There was more drinking and partying and purging the war from his system. It was time to feel alive; and not just for today but with the knowledge he was going to be here for tomorrow and many more after. It was time to celebrate and enjoy.

While in the euphoria of life he was also having a good time with a very attractive young lady that he had gone out with several times and kind of knew before the war. Well, at some point of decompression someone suggested marriage! And before you could say, 'are you insane?' or 'maybe we should sober up and think about this', they were on their way to Elkton, Maryland to get married. They headed to Maryland for the deed as you needed to be twenty-one in New York to marry and dad was still just twenty. Maryland was less strict on their age limits and were just as happy to bring these two lovebirds together in holy matrimony; or a civil ceremony.

Leave us just say that my father was not quite ready for the responsibilities and obligations of marriage. By his own admission the lady was serious and wanted to settle down into home and family, children, dogs and neighbors. My father was wild and couldn't seem to find the brake pedal.

It became quite obvious, within the first few months, this was not going to be marriage made in heaven. He was not working full time, and not at all some of the time, and hanging with friends. They were still carousing the same old places, doing the things they'd done to entertain themselves when they were kids last year. Drinking, singing and avoiding responsibility at all costs. She wanted to be an adult, to grow up, have kids, you know, actually have a life.

Then he and his friends decided they should head to Florida. First stopping in Tampa, where they had planned on finding work and, maybe, a liquor joint as a distraction, but things did not work out as they hoped. Prospects were slim for a bunch of rowdy Yankee boys down here and no one wanted them on their payroll. They decided to work their way down to Miami. Finding menial part time day labor on the way to pay for a sandwich and gas. Finally, in Miami they landed jobs at a hotel doing renovations. It was good work, but they soon got fired for unreliability. It would seem they found other things to occupy their time than show up for work.

They quickly found work for quick cash on a banana boat. What could be more fun than loading and unloading bananas in the tropics? It was hot, muggy, hard work with long hours and vile conditions. They were given the opportunity to see what being in a minority was like; as they were the only white boys working the boat. I'm not saying it was the same experience for them, working a few months on a banana boat, as it is for folks who live with that their entire lives; just a small taste. It would remain with him as a reminder his whole life. The shine came off the banana boat dream quickly and they realized it might be time to reassess their strategy.

It soon became apparent this was not a brilliant plan and it was time to head north, return to Williamson, and make right the mess he'd left behind. Within a few months of returning home they had the marriage annulled, she got her life back, my father took full responsibility for the failure and everybody moved on with their lives. They remained friends throughout their lives, with my mom and the lady involved actually becoming close friends. Probably because of the shared misery of being married to my pops!

It was becoming apparent that it was time to grow up and settle down. And in case my dad missed the signs, his father was more than happy to set him down and explain in minute detail exactly what that entailed. It was decided they would form a partnership, my grandfather would purchase a little over fifty acres of soy beans and my father would work it. Spending hours a day in the hot sun weeding, planting and harvesting should help keep my dad out of trouble. Plus, when he needed some extra spending money he could occasionally use grandpa's truck and haul whatever needed moving. They were successful on all accounts and the summer of 1946 seemed to be a turning point.

Fall arrived, and it was announced the American Legion would be sponsoring a semi-pro basketball team. Dad tried out, was picked and, once again, through hard work, diligence and willingness to put in the time, became quite a good ballplayer; a stand out on the team. It would seem his earlier talent for sports, and his time spent on the hardcourt during high school, had not completely left him, he loved playing ball. It was not just the time on the court but the camaraderie of teammates and a common goal. Success now came on many levels, basketball, the harvest and life turning around. After thrashing the beans, he now had enough money to buy himself a 1941 Hudson. He was once again styling and driving.

September 1946. A new teacher came to town to teach Spanish and Latin; her name was Carol Alliger. She was a city girl from up near Buffalo, come to the country to help instruct these farmers in the better side of life. She was young and pretty and my dad was going to meet her.

Williamson was a dry town so if the boys wanted to have a snort they needed to cross the town line to do so. So, a bunch of veterans would meet up at the soda fountain/ice cream parlor and then head off to one of the local watering holes just the other side of the town line.

My dad approached Carol about accompanying him to one of these roadhouses and she took one look at this farmer, in his bib overalls, looking like he'd just fallen off the back of a tractor and thought, 'he's nuts if he thinks I'm going to have anything to do with him.' And ignored his advances.

But, as there were not many entertainment options in a town like Williamson. You had Nick's soda fountain, Orbaker's drive in, for burgers and such, but she had no car, or reading. So, she began to show up at the basketball games for something to do. My dad was the leading scorer and kind of the star of the team and her attitude began to change; it's always the jocks, isn't it?

Once done with the soy bean harvest in the fall dad got a job driving the school bus for the winter and spring. Carol had taken up residence at a private home along the route and, as she had no car or other transport, would often ride to school on the bus, giving my father plenty of opportunity to begin to wear her down. He soon figured out he should not press as this was not your ordinary kind of girl he was used to impressing. She was smart, strong willed and needed to be won over, not sweet talked. They chit chatted most mornings on the way to school and he did his best to sound like an adult.

In March of 1947 near the end of the basketball season my dad was struck with severe abdominal pains. There were only two games to go until the season ended and he was determined to be there. He would find a way to put off dealing with the medical emergency until after the season.

Luckily, or, really, maybe not, he had a friend who he hung with and drank with who was a doctor. Dad put on his best schmooze and convinced the guy to give him some morphine pills just to get him through the last two games. He promised the doctor that as soon as the season was over he would get whatever was causing the pain looked at and taken care of.

The pills got him through the first game but the morning after he was in excruciating pain. His mother was very concerned. He looked horrible, washed out, bags under his eyes and he was in obvious agony. With a mother's perception she could see he was not well, there was definitely something wrong. She and his father would run him into town to see the doctor and if he couldn't see him they would head straight to the hospital in Sodus. He convinced her it was nothing, that he would be fine, just tired, probably something he ate after the game celebrating their win, he would go back to bed and rest. So, with reassurances that he would call a neighbor if things got worse, she and grandpa Z went to the movies for an evening out.

When they returned they found him passed out on the staircase. Ambulances were called, and a very rushed drive was made to the hospital in Sodus. He arrived alive, so they could perform emergency surgery in the middle of the night. His appendix had ruptured, and an infection set in. This was not good. After an all-night surgery and days in recovery, it would be a week before he began to come around to feeling human again. He could not eat and could not sleep without the aid of the morphine to kill the pain. It turned into a very rough recuperation, but he would live.

Interesting fact, though, was the doctor who'd been rushed in to do the surgery on his burst appendix was the very same doctor who'd patched him up after the car accident in 1941. Doctor Robert Harris. I am guessing he was getting tired of my father testing his healing skills and told him so. That meant dad had to begin to take much better care of himself and quit tempting the Grim Reaper. Our family is forever in this doctor's debt, twice.

Miss Alliger, the pretty school teacher came to see him several times while he recuperated in the hospital. As she still had no transportation of her own she took the bus over to Sodus to see him. Sometimes she could hitch a ride there with others coming to visit and then grab a ride home with either my dad's folks or one of the uncles. She was slowly becoming integrated into the family unit, whether she knew it, wanted it, or not.

Another few weeks recovery and it was time to find work once again. He found a job back working on a fruit farm, something he knew quite well as he had done this since he was a kid. And began to seriously start dating Carol.

Six weeks later they were married, June 7, 1947. Well, at least he had become less impetuous as he matured. The last marriage had come about on a whim during a drinking binge, this one he had waited six weeks and was sober; baby steps. None of their friends thought this marriage a good idea nor did any of them believe it would last. My dad had never met her parents and still was not a serious student of life. This did not bode well for the start of a life together.

They were as different as night and day. Dad was a strapping six foot one and mom swore she was an inch taller than five foot. No one would argue and try to take that inch back from her. He came from immigrant parents and poverty, she came from a family well established in the new world. Her great grandfather, McDermott, had emigrated to eastern Canada after running away from his home in Dublin as a young boy. He sailed the high seas throughout his youth, circumnavigating the world, finally settling in Kingston. There he acquired a wife, Mary Hagerty, from Cork, Ireland, and six lake vessels. He shipped lumber from the Georgian Bay to Tonawanda, making his fortune. An interesting side not, in my Grandmother's notes on this time period, she mentions he retired from the sea after 'many bouts with pirate ships.' Now, I do not know whether he was serving bouts on those ships or fighting them, but I do know once he settled in Kingston he was able to buy six lake vessels. Hmmm.

When he retired he sold off five of the ships and insisted on making one more trip. A storm kicked up, as they are wont to do on the Great Lakes, and he was reported lost at sea. A couple weeks later, my grandmother's brother Dick Webb saw his grandfather strolling down the street towards home. He was wearing a solid gold medal and chain given him by the Canadian government for saving the life of one Lt. Merrott. They are a very colorful family filled with artists, musicians, painters and oddballs. Sorry, great, great grandpa had made a lot of money, so they were eccentric.

My father's family began with nothing, made a little and lost it all, started a trucking business and went back to farming. They never made their financial fortune. They fought their way through the depression with little or nothing, earning every nickel they could to provide for the family. Mom's family had a maid and she was spoiled, (I say that with all the love in my heart and my father's, but facts are facts). She had never been in a kitchen, didn't know how to cook or clean or take care of a home. Dad had learned early on how to care for himself and help around the house, even learning to cook to a certain degree while he was struggling around the east coast. He told her none of that mattered to him, he loved her, and they'd work it all out. He wasn't marrying her for her cooking and cleaning, he was marrying her because he wanted to spend his life with her.

Impulsive is a trademark of this family. Impulsive and headstrong. Dad said he should ask my mother's father for her hand in marriage, he'd still never met the man. She replied that wouldn't be necessary as she knew what she wanted, she didn't need anyone's permission on how to live her life. That should have been a warning sign to dad that he might have a very, strong willed tiger by the tail but love is blind. So, they went to the minister's home, she didn't want a big deal, no big wedding, no huge reception with band and speeches. Just someone to witness, his brother Duane and his girlfriend Virginia, a judge or minister to speak the words and let's get on with life. Mom was a private person, the one thing they definitely had in common, not wishing accolades or recognition for what she was supposed to do. You had a birthday you got a year older, it was not a great accomplishment, everybody did it, she didn't want to be singled out in public.

So, the deed was done, she had written her parents earlier in the day, they would get the letter and knowledge within the next few days. And the folks high tailed it for Cooperstown for a night then on the New York City. They didn't have any money, so, found cheap lodgings not too far from the bowery and went out to celebrate. They found themselves in some dingy, dive bar, knowing no one. Everyone they told of this plan, the folks at the hotel and all, warned them against going to these places. Dad knew he could meet people and engage and they'd all be friends by the end of the first drink. They had a ball hanging with the hoi palloi of NYC! They were now man and wife and the rest would work itself out. They took a cab from the bar back to the hotel as apparently four tires were more stable than their four legs.

There is a famous story of my mother making a turkey dinner and leaving the innards in it and not cooking the bird long enough as well as moshing the side dishes. The honest portion of our story is, it was apparently the worst dinner ever prepared but my dad sat and ate it. He marveled at how good it was. She left the table in tears and shame as she had eaten some of it and knew the lie. Her cooking improved and the lying ceased...that's the story and I'm not one to argue with my father.

Within a couple weeks of their wedding day Carol was stricken with a very serious kidney infection and almost died. So, here they are, newly married, broke, a pile of doctor and hospital bills sitting on the table, assuming they had a table, and he had now lost his job. The fruit farmer needed him there for the season and my dad was running back and forth to the hospital to be with Carol. He missed too many days and the farmer had no choice, he needed someone he could count on.

The pressure was on and he responded by finding a job with American Roadways in Rochester. It paid more than he'd ever made before, he got overtime, and he was now getting a real taste of the trucking business.

The new job also made it possible for them to buy a house in Ontario, New York. Between the two of them, and a little begging and borrowing, they came up with the seven hundred dollar down payment and used his G.I. loan for the sixty nine hundred dollar balance on the house. It certainly wasn't a mansion, but it was theirs and the beginning of a new life. Though some furniture would have been nice. They had enough to sit on and sleep on, that would have to do for now.

Fall arrived and so did the opportunity for a job at Eastman Kodak, a job that was hard to come by as it was the place to work in Rochester. But luck was on his side and the job was his, life was certainly taking a turn for the good. To top it all off he still was able to play basketball and fastpitch softball in two different leagues as the schedule at Kodak was first shift allowing activities after work.

The following summer he was moved to nights at Eastman. Now, he and my Mom, spent their days picking sour cherries for extra money. Sports was put on the back burner and work was in the boiling pot up front. It was hard work, climbing ladders and filling bushel baskets with cherries, it was cold in the mornings and hot in the afternoons. He knew what he was getting into, he'd done this work before, but mom did not. She never complained, she just did the work and put in her full day. They could now afford some drapes and a few more pieces of furniture and decorations for the house.

In the spring of '49 he worked out a partnership with Homer Kiesinger to start Ontario Asphalt and Paving. He wanted to be his own boss, he'd worked for others too long, after all he was now twenty-four. The business folded in the late summer. Inexperience, luck, lack of knowledge and not enough of a cushion, hell they didn't even have a pillow case, to take them through bad times, was more than they could handle. Being your own boss was going to involve more than originally thought.

In September of 1949 they were to begin what would be a lifelong tradition, they moved. They decided to relocate to Tonawanda, New York. My mother's family all lived there and, as she was now expecting, she wanted to be close to them. The baby was due in December, she wished to be settled in well before that. Into a small, cramped upstairs apartment they moved. Again, it wasn't much but it was home.

It was probably not the smartest time to move. A baby on the way, a new town and no job; and jobs were increasingly hard to come by in 1949 with all the soldiers home and starting families and working. But once again fortune smiled on dad and he got in with the Chevrolet-Tonawanda engine plant. They found a small walk-up on Hill Street in Tonawanda, moved up, literally, in the world, and set down roots.

Bethann (Bitsy to those of us who knew her, then changed to Betsy in 1968 in college) was born 1949 and Chevrolet went down to four-day weeks immediately after. Things were about to get even tighter. As they had no hospitalization insurance, they had been paying the doctor a little bit every week before the birth of their daughter and then a little out of each week's paycheck after her birth. Now, they would have to do the same for the hospital. You win some and some gets taken away, it's called life.

It was becoming increasingly evident that if dad was to get anywhere in the world he was going to have to become better educated. He applied at the University of Buffalo in the spring of 1950 and was accepted under the G.I. bill. They would pay most of the tuition and books plus give him sixty-five dollars a month to live on, that would not be near enough to pay living expenses, hospital and doctors.

It was time to double team the work load. My dad found part-time work at the A & P Grocery. The cash would be necessary with a newborn and the ensuing bills, sixty-five bucks a month didn't go very far even back then, and he could still go to classes. He also had become very active in the American legion and worked on charity projects in his spare time. He was able to go in and clean the lodge on Sunday mornings for a little extra cash. It wasn't much but he was glad of the work, thankful to the American Legion for giving him the work and would sleep somewhere down the line. Every nickel helps when you are a young family. This would also become his M.O. throughout his life.

In early 1952 Robin, the eldest brother, entered the world. At the end of his college school year my father started working full time at the A&P and trying to go to school part time. Right at this juncture in life they needed money more than knowledge. He would get his education, it just might take a wee bit longer than anticipated. Also, with a growing family it became immediately clear that this cramped apartment was not going to suffice. It was time to buy another home.

Dad heard about a part time job opening nights at Associated Transport, a well-respected trucking firm up in North Tonawanda, so he applied and waited. But nothing came through. This would have been a good fit as his full-time job at the A&P was day shift and the part time trucking job was nights. And the extra money would certainly be welcome in the growing family. And he waited.

They did not call. A couple days later my dad noticed they ran another ad in the local paper seeking part time employees. Mom took the bull by the horns and called the company, demanding, in no uncertain terms, to know why they had not hired her husband-a very hard worker, a good worker-and yet were running ads in the paper once again. They told her to send him back over; dad returned and got hired on the spot. I think she scared them into it! Mostly, he worked on the docks but also drove truck on occasion. He was now onboard of the nation's largest trucking company.

Within days the folks at Associated began to recognize they had someone special. One of the other dockworkers proclaiming at one point that, 'if Bob couldn't lift it, it couldn't be lifted.' They called him Legs as he looked to be all leg and he never stopped moving, he was in constant motion loading and unloading trucks on second shift. He didn't tire, didn't take breaks and never appeared upset by the work, just seemed happy, smiling as he worked, to have the job.

A short few months later fortune would smile on my father; though fortunate for him not so for his supervisor. The man contracted pneumonia, so the terminal manger had to fill in while the supervisor recuperated. He noticed my dad and how he worked. After several days he popped in to the trailer dad was working and said, 'Legs, you seem to know what you're doing here. Why don't you come up to the office, so we can talk?'

In the meeting my dad explained that his father had been in the trucking business on and off for years. And he, himself, had worked for several companies along the line including Gravell's Express, a company that ran between Rochester and Oswego, plus he mentioned the job with American Roadways. He had been around a little at this point and, had to admit, he really enjoyed the trucking business.

The manager offered him a low-level management job in the office. It would mean a cut in pay but opportunity. Mom and Dad talked about it with the reasoning being that, yes, the dock job paid more, especially with the overtime, but that was all it was ever going to be. If he moved into the office, he might have an actual future with promise. They agreed, he would take the job. Mom would help with the bills by taking a job in a men's clothing store to help offset the loss of income. As a bonus, he, once again, was able to pick up part time work at the A&P, bagging and stocking. He was now the Assistant Dispatcher at Associated and a part-time bagger at the A&P, it was a start.

Luck and life would intervene once again when the head dispatcher made a costly error in allowing a driver on a dedicated run to come in several hours late. It caused all kinds of backups and slow-downs, loss of income for the company and the guy losing his job. They promoted dad. He was now the head dispatcher and moving in the right direction.

It would appear the decision to move from dock to office had been the smartest one he could've made, and he was now being rewarded for working hard, learning quickly, and doing a great job.

But not all was joy in the early 50's, life is a balance. As his career began to take off he was hit very hard by personal loss. His mother, Mattie, had gone into the hospital for a gall bladder operation. The operation had gone well but, as the grandfolks had no insurance, the hospital decided to release her early. She could recuperate at home. But a blood clot developed, unbeknownst to any one, and dislodged from where it was and flowed straight to her heart. She passed away at home. This was a devastating blow to all who knew her. She was loved and revered by friends and family alike, but it was overwhelming to her husband and sons.

Trucking

At the age of twenty-eight with a wife, a baby daughter and new baby son, after wandering in the vocational desert, spending a good deal of time discovering what he didn't want to do, he had whittled down his wants and needs. He had found a home in trucking, something he was good at and somewhere he looked forward to going to work every day. After almost dying a couple times in car accidents and hospitalizations, enjoying life just a bit too much, running away from whatever was on his tail, he had settled into life. He would not be a farmer or banana boat worker, he would not hold down a position at a factory or picking cherries, he had survived the war and its deprivations only to come home and deny himself nothing. Now there was more to work for, more important things in life, a family to focus on and a career to build. And he would build that career in trucking.

He knew this business. He had run routes with his father as a kid and had driven trucks and worked the docks on and off for a good portion of his life. He knew how hard the work was and what these men who did them were like. He knew the bitter cold of the docks in winter and the stifling heat in summer. Loading and unloading tons of freight every day for that paycheck. He knew them because he was one of them. Just a hard-working guy trying to support a family. And he would never forget that; he would never forget what that took or get above himself no matter how far he would rise in the industry.

They also continued to settle into the community, with my dad joining the American Legion in Tonawanda and taking on the responsibilities of First Vice Commander in charge of membership. His Sunday morning cleaning days were now behind him. He found he enjoyed being involved in community activities. Charitable work had its own rewards. It wasn't about the money or what it could do for him in the long run, it was about helping others. It was about the giving, he discovered the joy of giving without any thought of receiving in return. He never cared for unearned attention, felt uncomfortable when they would celebrate his birthday or some other occasion he had nothing to do with. It truly was better to give than receive. Including one time filling in as Abraham Lincoln for the Cub Scouts Memorial Day parade float when the real Abe couldn't make it. They had set down roots and were quickly weaving themselves into the fabric of Tonawanda.

This working-class town was home. Friends, family, roots and history. Yes, they were not exactly putting on the Ritz, no one they knew were, but they were getting by and the bills were paid. Everyone they hung with, all their friends and family were in the same leaky boat. They all knew and were there for each other.

Oh, there were glitches. Later in life and the marriage, now with four children, I'll tell you about them in a bit. It was somewhere around 1959 or 60 my dad decided he was going to take mom out for Mother's Day. They'd go to Del and Herb's over on Grand Island as they featured a wonderful chicken dinner. Mom wasn't sure they could afford such a luxury as they'd have to take all four kids and that could mean some money, money they didn't have. But dad assured her the kids would just order burgers and fries and they could swing it. You guessed it, all the kids order the chicken dinners. Dad was short. He either had to call his father in law, who now lived on Grand Island and knew everyone who lived and worked on the island or talk to Herb, and hope he understood. Of course, Herb had known the family for a few years now and he accepted my father's hangdog, embarrassed apology and promise of a return to settle the bill. The best laid plans...

Luckily for all involved hard work and a genuine enjoyment of the trucking business made the vocational rising come more quickly than originally thought. He was soon promoted from assistant dispatcher to dispatcher and, not long after I was born in 1953, he became the regional dispatcher. Associated decided at the time to move the regional office to Utica, New York. If he was to accept this promotion then it was time to move again, to leave all they had built in Tonawanda, in such a short period of time, and head to Utica. But when the chance for advancement comes you have to take it or opportunity will wave goodbye as it moves forward. My dad went on to Utica with my mother to follow.

My father commuted for several months while mom got all in order to move a five-year-old, a -two-year-old and a baby to a new home, not yet found, in Utica, New York. Betsy changed all those plans when she came down hard with the measles. It was more than just a case of the measles, she became sick enough mom couldn't take the chance on moving her and making things worse. And they had no idea how this would all turn out, they decided not to move from Tonawanda. They needed the support system intact.

Fortunately, with his work record as testament, Associated did not want to lose my father as an employee. In early 1954 they offered him a job as shift supervisor back at the North Tonawanda terminal. It wasn't the big promotion he wanted but he'd just turned that down for the benefit of his family. He was grateful they were willing to offer him anything, especially something that was a step up from where he had been. He gave it his all and learned. He would be promoted once again to operations manager.

They had bought a house just before I was born, and all the promotions began so the extra income was quite welcome. The bills had increased with a third child and new house, they just might make ends come close to meeting. Or at least passing in a darkened hallway.

With the help of a fifteen-hundred-dollar loan from my mother's folks-as they had just given her brother, Ike, the same, so all got the same-they'd bought the house at 168 DeKalb St. Tonawanda. This was a hallmark of both the Alliger's and Zonneville's, they believed that if you helped one child out, with a loan or a substantial gift, then you helped all children out with the same. Everyone got treated equally so there could be no accusations of favoritism. Or maybe they just didn't want to hear the kid bellyaching about mom or dad likes you better! Any who, The American Dream was being realized one step at a time.

Working six and seven days a week, even with the promotions, plus he was picking up extra work-he was still working part time at the A&P-they could soon afford a television set. Black and white, of course, as that was all there was as this time. Three whole channels of glorious black and white entertainment on from sunrise until midnight and then the sign off with the national anthem followed by the Indian head test pattern. And it was all visible on a massive 9" screen contained in a huge cabinet the size of a Buick. A 1953 Buick! Life, was good.

But, of course, life changes. The rain began in the early afternoon and kept coming. The wind kicked up as the sun went down and the rain kept coming saturating the ground. And the wind just would not let up. It grew into a huge storm, remnants of an Atlantic storm or hurricane, blowing through New York and the eastern Great Lakes in 1954. Between wind and heavy down pours the storm did heavy damage throughout New York state as well as to the neighborhood; including the folks new home. The tree fell, the damage done.

They had no insurance. The country and the economy were growing quickly in the 1950's, but paychecks still couldn't keep up the with largest surge in population, babies, homes, cars and their ensuing costs, in world history. The baby boomers were, well, booming. So, essentially you had a great many people purchasing houses and growing their families faster than their finances could keep pace with. Something had to give. Insurance premiums were not at the top of the necessity list. You didn't pay the money, you took your chances. They'd lost. But the guy who came to do the repairs knew the circumstance, he was in the same train car, and was willing to give them as much of a deal as he could as well as letting them pay some over time. It wasn't devastating, just more tightening of the belt.

In the spring of 1956 enter David, the baby, the third boy and fourth and last child of Robert and Carol Zonneville. The family was now complete, the house was fixed, the bills kept coming, they kept working and picking up whatever was available on the side to pay the increasing bills.

Children are a joy and a blessing that bring doctor and hospital bills, food bills, clothing and, sometimes, emergency medical bills. As it was for both Robin and David and, almost, back to back hernia surgeries, literally within months of each other. I'd had the mumps not long before and the bills kept coming. Even without emergencies children are not cost effective. There are shots, colds, flu, toys, shoes and food. And, ya gotta feed 'em.

One day dad came home between jobs to find the refrigerator had given up the ghost. They'd bought this in Rochester in 1948 and it had been a loyal member of the family ever since, now, it would appear, it was gone. Not what they needed on top of all else.

They called Sears and they sent out a repairman who pronounced the motor dead. They would need a new refrigerator. Damn! The repairman knew the feeling of this young family. He studies the frig and asks my dad where he bought it. Dad tells him Sears on Monroe Street in Rochester. Hmm, the repairman asks my dad if he'd be willing to pay the long-distance cost of a phone call to Rochester. Dad figures he's got nothing to lose and the call is made to Rochester where they are informed that they still have nine days left on the warranty. Nine days. So, the repairs are made with no cost. Sometimes it pays to be lucky.

From that moment on mom and dad never had any appliance in our house that wasn't made by Sears. It was because this repairman was willing to go the extra inch and make the call Sears now had a lifelong customer. Matter of fact I don't think I have ever bought an appliance or tool from anyone but Sears, so two lifelong customers. Service means so much.

Dad continued to work the two jobs at Associated and A&P sleeping whenever time would allow. Mom was working and going to school, she was going to finish her college degree for teaching, and we were kind of on our own a bit of the time. Not completely, mind you, but being watched by a father catching 40 winks on the couch allows for a certain amount of freedom. One day my mother came home to find all of us playing outside in the snow. We believed we were dressed properly for the occasion, jackets, mittens and scarfs, my mother disagreed. She was a great believer in heavy coats, boots and sweaters, to each their own. When asked where our father was we, of course, plead ignorance. She stormed into the house to confront him as to why his children were playing outside in the snow with no more than jackets on but could not find him. She searched bedrooms, basement, back yard, everywhere; no dad. Now anger was being replaced by concern and worry. We plead innocence. She was about to get on the phone to start calling all the usual places when from under our blanket and cushion fort, we excelled at forts of all kinds, there came the sound of snoring. We couldn't contain it any more and laughed uproariously. Mom, though I'm sure found the humor, did not let on. She awoke my father, who asserted he'd only been resting his eyes, and all were given a good talking to. You can't stay mad at a guy who is working himself to death to support his family.

Please keep in mind that between the years of 1949 and 1961 things were a bit crazy in the Zonneville house. They'd had four children, won and lost jobs, built up and paid down doctor and hospital bills, moved a couple times, dealt with childhood diseases and were working their tails off to climb the professional ladder. All the while going to school, working two or three jobs at a time and not sleeping or paying attention to calendars, so if some of this seems squished together and timelines skewed, it is because it all happened at once. But happen it did. Life doesn't wait for you to take notes and memorize dates, it keeps pitching, you keep swinging. If you remember everything that happened in your life and exactly when it happened, you weren't living, you were observing. And that's no way to live.

Things on the job front continued to improve. Hard work and a willingness to learn new things were paying dividends for dad. Associated had an employee they loved and were going to make sure he stayed. He knew the drivers, he knew all the dock workers and most of the folks in the office; and they knew him. It was obvious he was in this for the long haul and was going to remain in the trucking business. It was up to them to harness that love, that passion and allow him full rein to soak up as much knowledge and experience as he could hold.

The terminal manager at the time was not the strongest link in the chain and needed some assistance. He was not a people person, not someone who dealt well with the employees or the customers. More of a numbers guys and that did not translate to a business that was a handshake and a beer kind of relationship. Even at this level, it was personality even more than the bottom line for most customers.

Associated decided it was time to promote the old man again and made him assistant manager of the North Tonawanda terminal. He had the personality, he knew a good deal about the business, the other guy could handle the numbers, and dad could flourish in what he did best. He could learn those other details on the job. Though moving up further than assistant manager would be a problem as he had never completed college. And this was the new day, education was king, queen and the universe, you weren't going anywhere without it. All dad had was experience.

But the current manager was not doing the job. He was not respected by the people working for him or the customers. Dad knew everybody, and they knew, and more importantly, they respected him. He knew the business from the bottom up. He'd worked most of the jobs and knew them and what they took to do. That just might be better than a piece of paper from some college. The company wanted college boys, sheepskin in hand, whether they knew anything or not. One would have thought after having someone like that as manager they would see the book learning wasn't the be all and end all of trucking.

But they brought in a new manager, without offering the position to dad, who was much savvier than the last. This guy might have gone to college, but he knew the territory and the way trucking worked. Dad was able to learn a lot from this man and in the end the two of them worked well enough together it made the new guy look like a genius. So, within a short period the new manager was promoted and moved on to greener pastures. That meant the job was open once again.

This time they offered the job to my father. He had to think about it as he wasn't convinced he was prepared for this big a promotion. When you've been passed over twice for a job, and told you are not qualified because of certain shortcomings, you begin to doubt yourself; if even only for a moment. But he and mom discussed and decided the key to success is in the challenge, not the fear of the challenge; they offered, he accepted. It you are going to achieve in life you had to grab the bull by the horns when it came by, ready or not. He was now the terminal manager of Associated Transport, North Tonawanda.

By this time mom had received her teaching certificate and was now teaching in North Tonawanda as well, but she could not become tenured without a master's degree in New York. So, it was back to school nights while teaching during the day. After three years and a lot of hard work she received her master's from Buffalo State University. A mighty accomplishment while raising four children and working full time. It was the late fifties and they were on a roll. One thing my folks have never done, and no one in the family, as far as I can tell, is shy away from hard work or putting in the effort to accomplish their end.

Also, at this time Grandpa Zonneville had met a nice lady at the store where she worked. He had been alone for six years or so and craved some companionship. Hazel had never been married and welcomed his attention and advances. He was courteous, kind and treated her with respect. They hit it off, dating for a while before grandpa popped the question. She said yes, and they were married in 1959. Hazel was the only grandma most of us ever knew, as grandma Mattie had passed away when Robin was just a babe and Betsy was a toddler. She was the world to us. A wonderful cook, she filled that house with the scent of love from the kitchen, always welcoming and hugging when we would come for a visit. She would shoo us out of the kitchen with a large ceramic bowl and admonishment not to return to the house until all the greens were picked!

We would come back to the kitchen with our half-filled bowl

and present it to Grandma Hazel. "I know there were more peas and beans on the vine that this when I looked this morning," she would scowl.

"But that is all there is," we plead as innocently as four dumb, city children could. "Go check for yourself," we would say, "if you don't believe us."

"Oh, I don't have to look," she'd smile, "I know where all of them can be found!" she proclaimed. And then would poke our bellies, "you ate them all while picking, didn't you?"

She had us there. There is nothing sweeter, fresher, like garden candy, than fresh picked, right off the vine, green beans and sweet peas. We couldn't resist!

Hazel was, by all accounts, the best thing that could've happen in grandpa's life. She made him happy and took care of him right up until the time he passed. A lovely, self-reliant woman who, after grandpa passed and the 'boys' told her she could stay in the family house for as long as she wished, declined the offer. It had been 'his' house and she would not feel comfortable being there without him. She moved to a small place in Ontario, NY. They all stayed in close contact until she, too, succumbed to life. I always smile when I think of this fine woman.

Unfortunately, or fortunately depending on your point of view, due to his success as manager, they had increased sales and efficiency in North Tonawanda and were building numbers other terminals were having trouble keeping pace with. He was asked to pack up the family and move to Cleveland, Ohio. It was 1961 and we were being asked to leave our friends and all we knew so he could take over the Cleveland terminal and the sub terminal in Columbus.

None of us were happy to hear this news. Mom had all her family in Tonawanda and Grand Island, everything and everyone we had ever known was in this town. All our friends were there. But it was a nice promotion and a large increase in pay. Dad really had no choice but to take the job. Opportunity was becoming a regular at the door but that didn't mean it would continue. So, we moved to Euclid in March of 1962.

It was hard on everyone to leave. My folks had made friends who would remain so for the rest of their lives. Great people like Herb and Vivian Shamberger, Jim and Myrna Archibald, Loren, bones and Anita Hammett. And Kit and Pete Wilson. Dear friends whom we would know, visit and be close to throughout our lives. Even when Kit and Pete moved to Detroit, we would run up there for the weekend just to re-establish an old friendship! My mother's whole family lived in Tonawanda and Grand Island. Her folks, her brother and his family, aunts, uncles the whole crazy lot of them. Great Aunt Helen, she of the famous $50 bill she carried for years so she would never have to contribute to lunch. 'It's all I have,' she would mournfully utter. I think dad broke it for her in the mid-sixties, she could pay for her own sandwich from then on.

No more fun nights at the American legion or the Eldridge Bicycle club, Duffy Fangers or Skinny and Marie's. No more Sunday dinners at Grandma and Grandpa's on Grand Island. No more Warinski's hot dogs from Old Man River's. It was time to meet new friends and find new joints to hang at. Goodbye Dekalb Street, Hello 236th.

Adrian Zonneville

Mattie Zonneville

Frank Alliger

Ruth Webb Alliger

Z

JUL • 60
CAVS

Z

Robert

Duane

Richard

Allen

Paul Boesch (center, no hat) and the Boys

Adrian Zonneville

Hazel Zonneville

The Euclid Years Vol. 1

They rented the house at 1711 E. 236th Street for one year to get to know this new city and decide where they would settle. It was a two-story colonial with a nice yard, fenced in the back for Pandora. Two bedrooms up and one down, so the three boys would share one room and Betsy would get her own. Ah, the joys of being the only girl, the eldest child and of the elites!

They immediately discovered they had found the perfect neighborhood. Everyone on the street had found their way there by a circuitous route. They had moved to 236th from Virginia, Kentucky, Michigan, Mississippi and all points in between. Their names still taste so sweet on the tongue; The Chapel's, Parson's, Beacham's, Tarantino's, Sivic's, Hasse's, Thompson's, Modica's, Biddle's, Perry's, Quig's, Calvert's, Thomas's, Carpenter's, Bright's, Benedict's, Kosmetos, Midolo. I am willing to bet there is not a street you lived on in the past, that fifty years later, you can still name just about everyone who lived there. This was the tightest knit street any of us have ever experienced. And not just the street but the entire neighborhood. Within a few streets were the Blakemore's, Niccum's, Audia's, Zak's, all hanging together, helping when needed, providing support and friendship all the time.

The three boys would attend Glenbrook Elementary a half block away. In Tonawanda Mullen School had been almost half a mile form their house, though when walking with friends and farting around it was much closer. Betsy would attend Central Junior High, down the hill about a mile and a half. All was convenient, and you knew everyone in the neighborhood, in your class and the teachers knew you. Which was not always a good thing because that meant they knew your folks.

Of course, memory being what it is and siphoning out what it doesn't care to remember and magnifying what it will, this was an idyllic place to live. Across the street and behind the house was the school, the playground, tennis courts, a pool, baseball diamond and a couple of lovely gullies full of all kinds of things boys found to be marvelous.

But this was that kind of street, with kind and caring people who resided on that street. They were good people who wanted to raise their families and enjoy their friends. I believe it was my Dad, Bill Chapel and Bill Parsons who came up with the Idea of having the police close the street for a Sunday street party once a year. Everyone immediately thought this a fine idea. Barricades were put in place, tables and coolers brought out to the middle of the street, music blasted from homes and the party was underway. We don't know for sure what time it broke up as we kids had been in bed for quite some time. If they were waiting for one of the neighbors to call and complain so they would know when to call it quits, they were out of luck. All the neighbors were at the party. The police showed up some time in the night to collect their barricades, we assume the party had broken up by then.

There was the time, and I am a bit foggy on who started the ruckus, but either Chapel or Parsons was pulling out of their driveway. They lived directly across the street from each other and one of them backed-up up, just a little way, on the other's tree lawn. It was an accident. OK, it was a Saturday and maybe some alcohol had been consumed, maybe a beer, maybe two. Well, they started yelling, good naturedly, at each other, the crowd forms, no one was going to miss this show, and the next thing you know, Parson's, I believe, gets in his car and drives over to Chapel's yard turfing the entire front lawn. Chapel retaliates, and the next thing you know the brouhaha escalates and everyone is laughing, having another beer until these two knuckleheads spend their energy and shake hands. Quite the hoot.

There were also Bicycle rodeo's where all the kids from Glenbrook Elementary would compete and show off their bicycle skills and safety. They actually organized all the events, set up obstacle courses, and drew straight lines for us to ride down, all kinds of ways to test our skills for knowledge and safety. Afterwards the parents would show off their forgotten bicycle skills while they all hooted and heckled each other. For me this time period was the beginning of organized baseball, something I would love for life. All the parents came, coached, watched. The neighborhood was involved; the playground, pool and ball field at Glenbrook was our heaven.

As kids we ran free from morning until night, playing ball, riding our bikes, running around in the two major gullies out behind the school. My father would come out looking for us at twilight and we'd be playing ball. He would holler for us to come in stating there was no way we could still see the ball. I'd get a hit just to prove him wrong and he would sit and watch for a few minutes before calling it a game.

We lived across the street from our elementary school. You knew everyone who attended because they were all from the same neighborhood. Fights were confined to out behind the school, a few punches, a bit of rolling around on the ground and a handshake. I think this is why people always refer back to the fifties and early sixties as this idealized time in America. Those of us in the burgeoning middle class, springing up from those who had returned from the war, the G.I. Bill, the building of new industries, the highway system, the suburbs, were, for the most part, happy. Unions were strong, wages and benefits were good and America was on the move.

Of course, if you were darker in complexion this was not necessarily so. The pain and suffering of many, the discontent of the disaffected was hidden from view. No one talked about their feelings, women were happy with their lot in life and all was right with the world.

This, of course, isn't true but we wanted to believe it was.

It was the early sixties, and no one had shot JFK. No one was yet marching in the streets. No one was burning buildings and Viet Nam wasn't even whispered about let alone screamed. It truly was the end of a very short age of innocence for a large portion of America. A smaller portion, a darker portion, wasn't allowed that brief respite from the problems of the world.

Oh, we had to duck and cover and be prepared. But we didn't have to live with poverty or deprivation in our neighborhoods. Our parents weren't rich, but they were solid middle class, working, bringing home a paycheck each week. Food would be on the table and a roof would be over our heads, we didn't have those kinds of worries.

The folks and friends would get together for any occasion, football parties, cocktail parties, Memorial Day, Fourth of July and Labor Day, with volleyball, music, dancing, contests, limbo and twist, and a great deal of laughter. That was the one thing almost always present, the laughter and companionship.

On the job front all was chugging along with higher sales and lower costs at the terminal. Associated beamed in their brilliance of promoting dad even without a college degree. It turned out maybe having experience, real life, real work experience, was worth something after all.

Too many companies and organizations get caught up in the college trap. Not that going to school to learn isn't important, and well justified, but the problem enters when we decide to depreciate real life experience. We have concluded that a piece of paper far outweighs time on the job, Associated Transport, at the time, would disagree with that assumption when it came to my father.

Of course, it helped that he had be replaced another manager who was not well loved nor respected. The Euclid employees had been happy just to have a change of leadership. Once they discovered that dad had achieved his success due to earning it, and working almost every job on the way up, well, they were tickled. The fact he had done all these jobs earned him many points with those who still labored in them, they knew he would be tough but fair.

The customers took to him right from the start. If there is one thing-and there are a plethora- that my father excels at, it is meeting people and them taking to him. He exudes an energy and likability that is infectious. You just like the guy! Add all this together and you get great employee morale, increasing business, growth and more hours leading to more money in the everyone's pockets. People were happy. They knew he understood them and they were going to give him their all.

At one point the employees asked him to not only sponsor but join their softball team. Well, Dad the jock could not resist. He was playing in the outfield their very first practice. Someone hit a long fly ball, dad was chasing it down, but so was another outfielder, they collided, dad spent the next several weeks on crutches with a broken knee. So, ends the saga of my father's sport comeback.

Mom had landed a teaching job in Wickliffe, Ohio. She loved to teach and loved working with children, so she was quite content, and life had taken on a sense of comfort and effortless ease as days became happy years. E. 236th was as close to paradise as any street could be.

And my dad wanted to make sure mom knew how much he appreciated and loved her for making the sacrifices she had made throughout their marriage. Early on in the experiment in Euclid the Jay Cee's put on a style show as a fundraiser. Though dad was not an official member of the Jay Cee's everyone he knew was. I believe he was now beyond their age limit. It was and is, as far as I know, an organization dedicated to promoting young professionals and business owners. And if memory serves their age limit topped out at 35.

Anyway, at the show Louis Calvert, a neighbor and dear friend modeled this lovely navy-blue jacket with a mink collar. It was striking, and she wore it well. Mother could not take her eyes off it and talked about it all the way home. Dad, no slouch and observant as ever, got up the next morning and announced he had some errands to run. He would return.

He drove down to Gornik's Clothing, as sponsor of the previous night's event and spoke to Gene, the owner and friend. He explained what he wanted to do, purchase the jacket, and his lack of funds to do so. But he would give Gene a substantial down payment and do the rest over time. Understand this was before the advent of the omnipresent credit cards we have today. Very few people carried them back then and didn't want to. Cash was king!

Well, Gene had known dad for a few years now, he bought most of his work suits from Gornik's, and so he told dad he would give him a discount on the coat, as it had been used in the show. Dad asked what the discount might be. Substantial, it turned out. Though the coat was still going to set him back a dollar or two, it was mink, after all. My dad asked how they could set up the payments to which Gene relied, "Bob, just give me the money as you get it. Tell Carol to enjoy wearing the coat."

A good reputation and being a decent human being had paid off yet again. Dad thanked him profusely. Mom was flabbergasted, surprised and didn't have the temerity to ask how he'd afforded the coat. Until the day she died mom loved that coat

Oh, we still missed Tonawanda and our family back in New York. Everyone lived within a short drive of each other. And all were making their way in the world. My mom's folks were happily ensconced in the home my father had helped them build on Grand Island. Her brother, Ike, was a Sargent on the force in Tonawanda and the rest of the Webb's and Alliger's would never leave their childhood town.

Dad's brother's lives paralleled his. They gave of themselves to their country, got out alive and wandered in life for a short time before discovering what and whom they loved. But their successes shadowed dad's. They were lucky they found something in life they wanted to do, something they looked forward to going to every morning, and were able to make a living at it.

Duane had joined the Navy and served in the Pacific during the big war before returning to upstate New York and attending Cornell University. He graduated and worked at the Farm Credit Bureau, intelligently married Virginia, they had one the child, the golden child, Charlie, and was doing well professionally. Before Duane gave it all up to go back to school to learn the insurance business. He thought he might enjoy it a bit more that the credit bureau. He worked for a short time for Nationwide Insurance in Canandaigua before coming to the conclusion he would rather be his own boss. He quit the regular job to open his own insurance brokerage. He did well as he knew the products, the people and had a gregarious, wonderful personality. You could not be in a bad mood around Duane, he liked to laugh too much and would bust your nuts until you joined in. He was a joy.

Brother Richard served in the Army during the Korean war but was lucky enough not to have to go overseas. When he got out he also attended Cornell before getting a job at a bank down in Gainesville, New York. He was smart, personable, a Zonneville trait, apparently, people loved him, so, he quickly became the vice president of the bank and was set for life. Naturally, he quit and moved his family to New York City to learn to be a stock broker. He learned well, worked very hard and moved back to upstate New York, Rochester to be more precise, where he was once again extremely successful. He had found what he loved and put in the time and energy to succeed. Of course, early on he had made the wise decision to marry Martha who, like all the crazy ladies that married Zonneville men, supported him financially, emotionally and wholly while he pursued his dream. As did his four beautiful daughters, Annie, Sandy, Penny and Suzie.

The youngest boy, Allen, joined the Army and served in Korea. When that war ended he came home went to school and after a few stuttered starts and stops also fell into the trucking business. He got hired on with Consolidated Freight where he became the terminal manager in Elmyra and Syracuse, New York and then was promoted to the Akron, Ohio terminal. He was then promoted to Regional Manager in Birmingham, Alabama then took over all of Florida. He married Nancy, they had Lori and Jeff and later he married Betty. Things were going well for the Z's.

But as you can see, what was once a very tight knit family was splintering as success drew them further, geographically, apart. It seems for every success in life there is a payment, and ours was we no longer got together as we had when we were kids and lived within an hour of each other.

We would still try to meet once a year, usually at Duane and Virginia's as they had the most land. They had a nice house in Shortsville, New York; a rural burb of a few hundred just outside of Canandaigua. Their backyard abutted farmland. They had a huge yard where they could set up their huge tent for all the kids to 'sleep' in. I think the fathers had to draw straws to see which one had to sleep in the tent with the kids and corral them and try to force us to sleep; impossible. We were wound up from cases of Pepsi and too many hot dogs and hamburgers. Charlie had a pool table in the basement and minibikes, all kinds of toys none of city kids had. It was like our own amusement park.

And then there was the empty field across the street. Just the right size and dimensions for a ballfield. Had an infield and everything. So, the dads would play the kids in a ballgame. The four of them versus all of us. Now, keep in mind, all of the boys played organized ball, we weren't slackers. Really, most of the girls did as well. I believe all of Richard and Martha's girls played all through school. We had them well out numbered which only made the slaughter more embarrassing and painful. The absolute worse aspect of the loss is we knew they'd all been drinking beer most of the day and continued the whole time they were slaughtering us. They never set the bottles down, not even to bat. The fact they were half buzzed only solidified the humiliation. To this day when we get together that last game is always brought up. The old men never let us forget it.

It was a slice of heaven almost as delicious as 236th. But all things come to an end, even the paradise that was 236th. Bill Parsons got transferred to Buffalo in 1966. It was the beginning of the end. They had become fast friends, not only with the folks but everyone on the street, in the span of a few short years, and even though they would only be a few hours away, it was still disturbing when they left. It was breaking up that old gang on 236.

In 1965, early 66, Associated acquired Keystone Trucking in West Virginia and then Federal Express, a burgeoning company at the time, expanding their territory several times over. They had brought in a new boss above my dad who was a decent guy but really didn't know the trucking business. Obviously, Dad's duties were increasing exponentially, but his pay had not.

The new boss came to Cleveland in 1966 bringing his wife along and wanting to attend an Indians game. We love baseball in this family, so this would not be a chore. After the game Dad and he were enjoying a cocktail and talking when dad brought up the subject of his pay and the increase in workload. The regional manager asked what dad thought fair compensation would be. Dad gave him a number and he agreed. The raise should cause no problem and as the head of the company was impressed with what my father had accomplished, the guy could see no reason he would object.

Dad explained that he knew all pay changes had to go through this same head of the company and he was known for taking forever to do so. Dad was not going to wait forever, they had until the beginning of the year to make the change or he would be gone. Not to worry, was the reply. Not worried, said dad, just stating the facts.

October 1st comes, and dad makes the reminder call. Not to worry! End of the year arrives, and dad decides he will take all of us to Florida to visit the maternal grandfolks and a ten-day vacation. Why not? Either he is going to come home to a nice raise or not. We might as well enjoy one more trip on Associated, paid vacations are swell, before we returned to find out whether dad had to quit, and we were moved back to poverty, or life would be flush.

We returned December 31. The next day dad heads into work, a holiday, to pick up his check; which they always left in his desk drawer. It had not been changed. The following day, the first official work day of 1967, he called and asked how much notice they needed; he was leaving.

"Why?" Stammered the boss.

"I told you in June what I needed and what I would do if the raise didn't happen, it didn't happen, so how much notice do you need?" No sense beating around a bush that wasn't there.

"30 days."

"OK, you got it."

That evening he received a call at home from the president of the company telling him all would be made right. But my father would not back down, stating, "if I have to resign in order to get a pay raise then I don't want to work for this company. It shouldn't take that."

The president reiterated they would need the thirty days and my father agreed, he would stay. He was then asked if he'd found a job yet. No, but he knew he would. You got to have confidence, boy, if you ever want to succeed!

Within a few days Spector Motor freight offered him a position with a higher pay increase than Associated had offered when he was quitting. His last day with associated was February 7th, he was on the pay role at Spector February 9th. He had landed on his feet once again. Truly the luckiest man I know; though sometimes luck is found in hard work, reputation and a willingness to take the chance.

Sometimes we jump from the bridge without knowing what, if anything, awaits below. My father took the plunge without any guarantee of another job. But he believed. He believed in himself, his skills, his experience and, maybe, just a little blind faith. As his brothers had believed when they made their jumps from security to unknown territory.

And Spector had made the right choice as well, proven by his performance, quickly increasing sales and cutting costs once again. All without irritating unions or office workers. Things were definitely on the upswing.

It should be mentioned that the employees of Associated gave him a huge send-off party. Office workers, drivers, dock workers all contributed to a set of luggage and other gifts to show their appreciation for what he had meant to them. These were people who had pulled together, worked hard, increased business and meshed as a group. They were close and very sorry to see him move on; though they understood why.

As a matter of fact, not to brag, but Spector was soon so happy with the job he was doing in Cleveland that they had him running up and back, several times a month, to straighten out the Detroit operations.

He had only been with Spector a few days before his first test would come. The only person he knew was the regional manager who'd hired him. He had not had anywhere near the time to establish relations with other employees up and down the corporate or hourly ladder. But he had a reputation in the industry as a man who was fair and honest with all employees; not a just a corporate climber but someone who cared.

Quickly came the day the vice president of the teamsters called to let dad know that he, personally, would be coming to meet as there had been a problem and no one seemed to care to take of this problem. He was going to see it solved. He made no bones about his displeasure. Apparently, a guy who enjoyed flexing his muscle and letting those in charge know he would not lay down or be subservient. All of which caught my father by total surprise; he'd only been at this job for a few days. Time to find out what the hell was going on before this union man arrived.

He called in the office manager and grilled him about what might have upset the union so. The office manager explained that a supervisor had called people in for overtime a while back but had not bothered to check the seniority list. He had missed a few of the more senior guys and they'd not gotten the choice of overtime. When my dad asked why they hadn't simply paid the men for the shifts they missed, as it was the company's screw up not the employees, the manager replied he was worried about the home office and their reaction. This guy didn't want to lose his job and didn't want to bother those with the power to do so.

I believe my dad said something about the hell with the home office, pay the men what they were owed, and he would deal with the higher ups. If a mistake has been made it was up to those who made that mistake to make it right.

The next day, right on time, the vice president of the teamsters strolled into my dad's office accompanied by one of his agents. He immediately stated that he was going to shut down the operation as these claims were well past due and they had not been addressed. And the terminal would remain shut down until all had been resolved! Apparently, strong arm tactics were his M.O. Dad got up from his chair without a word, put on his hat and began to don his coat.

"Where are you going?" asked the hard-edged union man.

"Well, if you're going to close us down, I'm going out to get myself a nice lunch." Responded my father. "If there is nothing to discuss then I have no need to be here." He continued to put on his coat.

The teamster VP calmed down, helping my dad out of his coat and expressing his desire to talk and work out whatever they needed to. He stated he knew my dad was new at Spector and was certain he would want to get off on the right foot and work with the union over here. But he knew my dad's reputation and expressed that he knew dad didn't react impulsively like this, there must be something they could work out together.

My dad then explained that the claims had been handled. The office manager, who had been quietly watching dad work his magic, now showing the teamster all the paperwork attesting to said claims. They shook hands, proclaiming they would work together for the benefit of all. Dad did not suffer intimidation or threats, nor did he suffer fools who used them.

Dad had been in the trucking industry for more than a decade and a half now and he was good at this job because he loved the business. If you truly enjoy what you do, can't wait to get to work in the morning, more than likely you will excel at your chosen profession. He did. And he would not be chased around like a frightened girl because the union or the president himself was doing the chasing. He stood his ground, did what was right by all and could not be intimidated.

Now he was able to increase business and payloads quickly. He got along famously with the customers and with the workers. He set goals and they did their absolute best to achieve; as they were rewarded for their efforts they really wanted to please my dad. They wanted him to succeed because they knew his success would be theirs as well. More jobs, more hours, higher pay.

He challenged his sales people and operational department early on. He sent out a challenge on the teletype, not just to his people but to every office across the country as well as headquarters. It was a simple statement; 'I do not know who is number one in growth in Spector, but you better get out of the way as we plan to be number one!'

The call came immediately from his regional manager wondering if he'd lost his mind. As well as explaining, in very colorful language, what a lot of nerve dad had. Did he realize what a risk this was? Did he understand how this would look? How this might affect morale if they failed? He was informed my father had no intention of failing and neither did his crew.

The regional manager informed my dad that once a month all the regional managers and the home office had a conference call on a Saturday morning. Just the regional managers not my father or any other terminal managers. It was a once a month telecom on how the company was doing and what they could do to improve business. Though my father was not invited to participate his manager said he was going to give dad the code, so he could call and listen in the next conference call. He would hear for Himself what those above him thought of this prank. He was instructed not to say a word, not to breath hard, just listen lest someone on the call hear him.

Saturday morning came, and dad was on the phone, quietly listening. The Executive Vice President came on the line and stated that, though he had not met this new manager in Cleveland he was going to make it a point to do so. What this guy has done, challenge the entire company while only being on the job for a month was audacious. And he plans to do all this was, well, 'unbelievable'!

Well, the die was cast, and it was time to put up or shut up. Everyone got into the competition, dispatch, sales, dock and drivers, operations and management, they were determined to show they could accomplish the Objective. Just before Labor Day, seven months later, they had done it, they were the number one terminal in the country. They could rest on their laurels.

They could have but my dad was not in a resting mood. Labor Day week was, of course, a four-day week due to the holiday. But my father told anyone who would listen they would do a regular week's revenue. Several of his key people took him aside and quietly insisted he may have lost his mind and might have set the goals too high this time.

Dad got on the phone calling a couple of their largest customers and explaining the situation. Even the customers loved this idea, they loved that he was challenging his employees to go above and beyond.

They told him send along some extra trailers to their plants. They would be working over the weekend, if he'd send the trucks they do all they could to fill them. On the Sunday of Labor Day weekend, they called him at home to let him know they needed more equipment. Dad called in more drivers and the ones that wanted the double overtime came in and provided all that was needed. Double time is a lovely incentive. They wound up surpassing a normal week's revenues in four days. All had done more than what could be expected, and they had prevailed, there was excitement and a celebratory feeling throughout the terminal. A triumphant party was in order, all would get to relax and enjoy the fruits of their labors all on the boss. Well, fruits, hops, grains, barley and some food; these folks knew how to enjoy life!

If memory serves, the Spector terminal was at 79th and Kinsman. That was ground zero during the Hough riots. Due to economic and social conditions at the time, and for a couple centuries before, the east side of Cleveland, as well as many large cities at the time, exploded in anger and violence. Black folks had had enough promises and empty hands. They wanted equality, they wanted jobs, they wanted their piece of the American pie and if they couldn't have it they would make damn well sure no one else was eating at the table. It was time of unrest, mistrust and anger.

My father was determined to keep the terminal open and operating. The police did not have the manpower or training to quell the rising violence, looting and fires. Thousands rioted in the streets and they would not be quelled with words and empty buckets of promises again. So, the National guard was brought in to restore peace. Armed troops patrolled the streets of Cleveland as well as Los Angeles, Detroit, Philadelphia, Chicago and other major cities. It was a time of upheaval, discontent and demands for equal opportunity and treatment.

My father had become known as man who didn't look at the color of your skin but whether you wanted to work. Whether you were willing to come in and bust your butt for a paycheck. At one time several members of a civil rights organization came in to demand that they hire more black workers. My dad responded that if they wanted to work they would be hired and treated the same as everyone else. He didn't put up with disruptions, at work or at home, and all were welcome. He also didn't put up with white workers giving black workers a hard time, if you worked, you all worked together. This was known throughout the neighborhood, the people respected him and the business.

The evolution of the Zonneville family's awareness, growth, empathy and understanding of others continued. My grandfather had come over from the old world with old world opinions, he was not the most enlightened individual when it came to people of other colors. He would not talk to me because I had a 'gook' name; Kim. It is funny because my Uncle Al said much the same thing as he had just come back from fighting in Korea and was surprised by my parent's choice of name. We would make many jokes about it later in life. We became quite close over the years. But my father had grown well beyond those concepts. He would pass his 'liberal' views down to his children who would, we hope, continue to evolve on these and many other issues.

My dad would go to work every day, through the rioting and violence, clear himself with the National guard surrounding the area then come home at the end of the day. Only to turn around several hours later to go back to the terminal to make certain all the employees working at night were safe and well. As he says, they had several women who worked at night and he wanted them to know they were safe. They hired several armed guards to patrol the grounds just to back up the Guard outside. It was a dicey time in American history.

During all of this turmoil Spector asked my dad to travel to other spots on the map to run training classes. One of those spots was Milwaukee, Wisconsin. He had no inkling that very shortly he would be offered the Regional Manager position out of Milwaukee taking charge of Wisconsin, Minnesota and Northern Illinois. Another promotion, another move, another change.

On Wisconsin

Our short time in Euclid had been fruitful and happy. We all were to make friends who would remain so throughout our lives. Dad had, in his usual fashion, joined the Elks lodge and thrown himself full into it. He didn't believe in joining an organization just to join, just to make contacts. If you joined a benevolent organization, you got in all the way. He became Chaplain, Lecturing Knight and finally Exalted Ruler of the lodge. They raised money for those with special needs, Scholarships, Scouting, Veterans programs and just a bunch of do-gooding in general. They had fish fries and Friday dinners, we went to them all. It was a good group of folks all joining together to help others.

He also took over the loose organization of home owners in and around 236th as well as becoming active in the Presbyterian Church becoming not just a member but an Elder. Dad never did anything halfway, if you join, you join wholeheartedly.

They also frequented the Euclid A club down the hill. A local joint that featured great home cooked food and cold drinks. Just in case you were wondering whether these people had any fun while saving the world. Yeah, in between all the good works and church they managed to enjoy themselves. Many of the block parties, backyard parties, party parties all featured homemade food, music and beer; and booze.

But it was time to head towards the new life in Wisconsin. First

Betsy had to graduate from Euclid High School, from there she was to attend Bethany College, in Bethany, West Virginia, my mother's alma mater. Now, the move to Wisconsin threw a monkey wrench in that plan. She didn't want to be that far from the folks her first year in college.

Dad pulled some strings and with the help of Roger Gerling, Executive V.P. of Spector, she was able to transfer over to University of Wisconsin, Madison. Sometimes it pays to know the right people who can pull the right strings.

Dad commuted between Milwaukee and Euclid from April of 1968 until June when they sold the house at 1711 to Gene and Bea Burke, my math teacher at Central. Dad had found a home to rent on Walters Court in Elm Grove, Wisconsin. Mom came and gave her approval. We, were not consulted. Though we heartily approved. We didn't quite fit in to the high society of Elm Grove. This was a fairly wealthy suburb of Milwaukee and we were far from wealthy. Dad just got a nice deal on a beautiful home that they rented for a year. It was a really nice house.

Four bedrooms up and a master suite on the first floor. There was a small library/den, a family room, formal dining with a stone fireplace you could, literally, walk into, a beautiful large kitchen with walls of windows to look out on the acre of wooded lot. And a finished basement with a ping pong table already in it! Heaven! It was wonderful! We all got our own rooms, first and last time that would happen. Well, until we moved out on our own.

And the Grades lived next door! Jack Grade was a doctor. He and Shirley had eleven kids, so there was someone in the family the same age as each one of us. We never became close friends with the Grade kids, but mom and dad did with Jack and Shirley. Jack had been the team doctor for the Milwaukee Braves and was, therefore, a great sports fan. He and dad were set. They went to Marquette Basketball games, Packer Football games as well as baseball games. They might have shared a few martinis along the way as well.

The folks and Grades would head down to the Elm Grove Inn, owned by Al McGuire, the Marquette basketball coach, for vittles, cocktails and talk of sports, life and laughter. It made things bearable for mom who missed Cleveland and the 236th Street gang. As far as I can remember the Grades were the only true friends the folks ever had in Milwaukee.

Tonawanda had been home for mom. Her family was well established there, had a history there. Her grandfather, on her father's side, had been the first mayor and had come from money. He had set a land speed record in an automobile from Buffalo to Rochester. They were known, both the Webb's and Alliger's. Hell, there's an Alliger Street in Tonawanda. Both sides of this eccentric family had deep roots throughout the area. The Webb's were known due to the wealth created by their grandfather of shipping fame as well as the fame his grandson's, Harry and John, had created on the Vaudeville circuit. They toured the country, headlining theaters and fairs. They never made a ton of money, back then even the main acts struggled to pay their rent and food, but they did collect stories. Many of which I listened to at uncle John's knee when I was but a wee lad.

They had a singer try out to join Webb's Entertainers in Seattle. He was good, according to John, but they didn't need him as they were already headliners. Why give up another piece of a dwindling pie? His name was Bing something. Oh, Crosby, I believe. They used to collect bedbugs and such in glass containers to take home to their mother just to freak her out. Boys will be boys, no matter the age. They played all the top theaters from coast to coast until they just couldn't anymore. We actually found a recording they did in 1921 called 'Old Man Jazz'.

Our neighborhood was young families just starting out. They had much in common and shared interests. We knew the folks and kids who lived around us. If you got hurt or needed something and it was during the day you went to Mrs. Gerke's house. Your folks were working, she was home. It was a neighborhood.

236th Street had been a community bonded by similar interests, family, friends, sports, charities and love. You knew everyone on the street. It was THE neighborhood. It was family. These were new families establishing themselves in the world. It was a more mature crowd agewise than Tonawanda, though not by much. There was enough immaturity and youth running through the veins to keep it fun. Lives were woven with interests in jobs and charities and children. It was tight.

Nowhere we lived in Milwaukee ever felt like that. Nowhere could live up to what we had on 236th at that time. We knew a couple folks on the street, the Grades and such, but none would ever be as close as the gang in Euclid. 236 was like its own village. Everyone watched out for each other, they were there if you ever needed a hand or a tool. If you needed an ear or someone by your side while life hit you hard or you lost a loved one. You would never be alone, you would never be allowed to suffer life's slings and arrows by yourself. Someone had your hand, your heart, your back. The bar was set impossibly high.

All the kids played together and knew who to come to if the folks weren't home and someone got hurt. You just can't replace that. And mom grew lonely and missed that companionship. She never really took to the towns of Elm Grove, Brookfield or Milwaukee. She didn't hate them, but she never loved them.

They attended church up the street. It was Methodist, close to home, less than a half block away, walkable, even in inclement weather. And the minister would have early services during football season so no one had to miss the start of Packer games. He knew his crowd. The folks would go to some of the better German restaurants in Milwaukee, Karl Reisch's and Mader's. They had a Strawberry Schaum Torte that was to die for.

Even with all this I believe my sister and I were the only ones in the family who enjoyed the Milwaukee era. I came of age, joined a band or two, hung out with people I should've stayed away from, got my driver's license, got in trouble, went to concerts with my sister and her boyfriend Bob, got involved in the anti-war movement, got classified as 4-F for the draft and generally had a great time. Bits went to college, loved the atmosphere, the learning, being surrounded by people who craved more, met the love of her life, the same Bob from before, wound up getting her named changed to Betsy by her first roommate and generally had a good time. The rest of the family, not so much.

Dad was on the road most of the time between covering

Wisconsin, Minnesota and overlapping areas. At the end of 1968 he was called to the home office. Time for another promotion and a raise and more territory. They added Chicago, Northern Illinois and parts of Iowa. He would be gone more and working more. Such is the life of the trucking company. The threat of 'wait 'til your father gets home' was losing more traction every day.

As it appeared we were now going to be setting down more permanent roots in the Milwaukee area they purchased a home in Brookfield; the town that surrounded Elm Grove. It was a bit more blue collar than Elm Grove and more suited to those of us from sterner stock. We would be staying in the area. Not good news for Mom, Robin or David but it didn't break my heart. They joined the Oconomowoc Country Club as a way to meet new folks while they played golf and dined. None of it filled the void.

Midway through 1969 Spector Motor freight underwent reorganization and Dad had another new boss. They brought in John Bresnahan from Consolidated Freight. There would be shake ups. In October he came to my father and asked him to, once again, relocate. They wanted him to take over a new territory they were creating but told him not to discuss or even mention this change to anyone as they were still working out details. He couldn't even mention to his family.

Life can be series of defining moments, sometimes great, course altering, sometimes things you have nothing to do with. Some of my father's were both. Two crossings of the Atlantic. The first a western crossing that would redefine the history and the future of the Zonneville family. Something my father had, obviously, nothing to do with but it would lay the course for his life. The second an eastern crossing taking him back to Europe and the war. He lived through that war, up close and personal as well as the depression. He was literally up to his chin in both.

But on July 16th, 1969 he, as was every other person on the planet, was part of a defining moment for humanity. We sat and watched a human being set foot for the first time on an astronomical body some quarter-million miles from Earth. Obviously, dad had nothing to do with the moon landing but imagine, if you will, a person growing up in a home with no electricity and heated by a stove, going to an outhouse, walking miles to school, sometimes riding horses and here he sits in his living room, watching on a color TV, a man walking on the surface of the moon. If you ever wanted something to prove all things are possible, I can't think of a better example. Life was laid out like a banquet before him, he just wasn't sure what the menu would be.

He heard nothing for months and chose not to ask about it. It had been long enough, he considered it a dead issue. It was just as well he'd never brought it up to Mom or us as it would've only created turmoil he didn't need right then. He no longer had to concern himself with moving again. Then on December 23rd the boss called him and said to come to Chicago for a meeting. At the meeting he was told the move was on. He would have to go home and tell the family.

He drove back to Brookfield and had a family meeting, explaining he'd been offered a new region the company was putting together but it meant they would have to move again. He knew they wouldn't like it, but they didn't like Wisconsin either; well, except for Kim and Betsy. When they asked where there were headed next, he informed them his new territory would encompass New York, Pennsylvania and Ohio. They would be moving back to Cleveland. OK, he played it for all it was worth knowing they would be overjoyed to be heading home. He would have to report to Cleveland on January 3rd. They would come as soon as they sold the house and could pack up.

He had delivered the greatest Christmas gift ever, wrapped in joy and a great big bow on top!

When dad headed to Cleveland in January Robin went along. He split his time between the hotel with dad and the Chapel's new home on Edgecliffe, so he could, once again, attend Euclid High School. He then would get to graduate with the people he'd grown up with in Euclid, his friends and schoolmates for most of his life, rather than the people he hardly knew in Brookfield. All were happy.

Once again March came and once again we moved. I don't know what it is about the month of March for my family, but we seemed to move the most in March. I believe it had something to do with trying to get us in a school before the end of the school year, so we could meet and make friends. The hope was to make summers less lonely.

Of course, dad said we could live anywhere in Cleveland we chose as he would continue to be on the road most of the time. Though the terminal he would be working out of was southeast of Cleveland itself; actually, in Cuyahoga Falls, but we would choose.

My dad was on the road when he received a call from Madeline Beacham. She'd heard through a very powerful grapevine that the family was going to move back to the Cleveland area. She asked if he might be interested in returning to 236th street. Of course, he would! Well, Chapel's old house was up for sale. She knew because she still lived next door and the guy had made it known to her he was leaving. And soon! If dad could get back to Cleveland right away she was sure the house would be his.

Dad finished his business in Rochester hopped in the car and hightailed it back to Euclid. One has to strike while the iron it very hot and he was in a striking mood. It was dark when he showed up on the doorstep of 1720 E. 236th Street. But not late. Though what concerned him was there were no lights on in the house. Well, nothing ventured, nothing gained. He knocked.

A middle-aged man comes to the door and my father explains that he heard the house might be for sale and wanted to know if it was true. Yes, the fella needed to sell right away as he was headed to California. He couldn't show dad the house as the power was out right now, so he would have to take his word for the condition of the home. Dad asked if anything had been changed since this fellow had bought the house from Chapel's, and the answer was no.

Dad knew this house, we all did, we had been in it hundreds of times and loved it. I was similar to the house across the street where we'd previously lived except this house had a large family room on the back and a swimming pool. We knew this house and dad wanted it. The fella explained he had to leave for California in the morning but if dad could come up with $1,500 that night they could seal the deal. Dad went to the hotel made a hurried phone call or two to old friends and begged and borrowed, he soon had the cash in hand. Now they needed some kind of contract.

This man goes inside the dark house rustles up an old, used envelope. He brings it to the door and they scribble an agreement on the envelope, $1,500 down and dad would assume the mortgage of $26,000 through a G.I. loan. Both sign on the invisible dotted line, contract! All done he heads back to his hotel out on Euclid Avenue.

He is up at the crack of dawn to go to the bank, envelope in hand, to legalize the deal. Dad was not going to wait an extra second, he was there as they unlocked the bank doors. He would make this deal go through if he had to pull it with a semi. The banker can't believe the story he is being told but admits the envelope is binding. So, he notarized the envelope, gives dad the loan and transfers the money to the other guys account. Done! The house is now mom and dad's, though mom doesn't know this yet.

He calls her and tells her he has purchased a home. She is not pleased. He has never purchased a home without her approval before. He appeals to her good nature and says he honestly believes she will approve. Come to Cleveland.

Dad drives out to pick her up at the airport that afternoon. He shares small talk and chit chat about this and that, everything but the house. But, she noticed as they are driving she recognizes more and more of the surroundings. They pull up in front of the, formerly, Chapel house and he stops.

"What do you think?" he smiles.

Mom had always loved this house. It was everything she could ever imagine where she would live for the rest of her life. She was OK with the purchase.

Another day later dad comes by to see something taped to the door. A summons. What? Dad has to go to court to straighten out whatever needs straightening. Apparently, the guy in question had screwed someone on some kind of patent deal and he was skipping the state before the law could find him. He had also stayed at the same hotel the night before he left as dad had. The judge was now accusing my father of colluding with this man. And was looking at jail time. My father pulls out the envelope, explains exactly how the deal went down and all involved. The judge, stymied by this story, says, “nobody could make up a story so convoluted and unbelievable. I believe you.” Case dismissed. The house is theirs. He should have framed the envelope and hung it on the wall.

Stan Biddle came down to help clean up and paint and help them move into their dream home. This house was just so much nicer than the house directly across the street where we had lived two years ago. It had the nice back family room and a pool. Yeah, we now had a party house. Mom was overjoyed and announced, ‘We are back home.’ And it was 236th!

The Euclid Years, Vol. 2

We had returned to the loving embrace of our favorite street. Back amongst old friends, and cohorts-family, really. Back to the Beacham's, Chapels-who maintained their ties with the old neighborhood as they were only a few miles away-Hasse's, the Calvert's, the Biddle's, Perry's, all of that old gang. We were well and truly home. Robin graduated from Euclid High School in June of 1970.

This is where things get a bit screwy for my father and me. Our relationship never became estranged just a bit strange.

First off let me say that both my brother Robin and I finished our high school careers the same year; he in June of 1970, I in November. I had gotten involved in the anti-war movement back in Milwaukee and brought that with me to Euclid. That, and an aversion to authority figures that bordered on neurotic, combined with the natural insanity and anger of teen years and it was a recipe for trouble.

I'd left my love for sports behind when I began to play music in 1966. As I mentioned earlier I had gotten involved in and with some folks who may not have had my best interests to heart. I was a little crazy and my father, well, neither of my folks, appreciated my course in life. But he was gone most of the time and I was without direction. The only thing I knew for a fact was I was pissed off at just about everybody from the president on down to many of my classmates. Whom I thought less than whole or smart because they were not involved, nor did they care, about the war, the draft or trying to make the world a better place.

I do not blame his absence, I do not blame anyone or anything. It was who I was and still remain to a certain extent. I still see most authority figures like a bull sees red. There just seems to be something in my DNA that rebels. My sister used to refer to me as a hippie on a self-destruct kick. She is probably right.

When they threw me out of high school my father was given the chore of taking me to juvey hall. This would not be pleasant half hour drive. Silence wrapped the car like a suffocating blanket as we drove down the Shoreway. The sound of the tires on pavement drowned out any hope I would live past the chiming of the next hour on the clock. As we got close to 55th street, he glared straight ahead as he said, very quietly, "well, you screwed up this time," here we go. "Here is what I am going to tell you, you don't ever have to get married, live in a nice house, drive an expensive car or have kids, as far as I'm concerned. There is one thing you do have to do and that is work for a living. You have messed up many of those options with this, this stunt, but you can still succeed. Find something you love. Don't worry about the money, never work for money when you don't have to, work because it brings you satisfaction and joy and you'll never work a day in your life."

"I want to play music, I want to be a performer," I stated.

"Find something else," he mutters as we arrive at Juvenile Hall.

Though if push comes to blame, the folks have to take some kind of responsibility for my choice. Bob and Carol Zonneville loved music. Not always the same genre, they had come from completely different backgrounds and upbringing, mom from wealth, dad from dirt poor farming. They were as different as night and a sunny mid-afternoon when it came their sampling of art, music, and literature.

Mom came from a family of cultured, musically educated performers, players and devotees. Her uncles had toured the Vaudeville circuit for years in the teens and twenties. Admittedly playing that wild new jazz of the time but also throwing in some classical for flavor. We have one of their recording from near the end of their musical career. It's a hoot.

Dad loved Country. He enjoyed Western, but he LOVED country. Kitty Wells, Loretta Lynn and Patsy Cline. Johnny Cash and Earnest Tubb. All the Hanks, Thompson, Snow and, of course, Williams. He would rise early of a Sunday morn and throw on a stack of records three inches thick, crank up the stereo and start to cooking. Eggs and ham, sausage patties and potatoes, toast and pancakes, it was a spread that would put any diner to shame. You would awaken to the sound of some hillbilly howling his grief about a "Great Speckled Bird" or a "Six Pack To Go", and you knew what day of the week it was. It was dad's day and there would be sorrow and grief and a hootenanny this morning. It was wonderful.

Mom loved classical and jazz. She played the piano, all were required to learn an instrument in her family, though she was the only one who stuck to it. We inherited a baby grand piano from her mother, who'd inherited it from her mother, a Steinway, not a Steinway and Sons, but a Steinway. I believe my sister is now the keeper of the keys. (yes, it was a long way to go for that!) Mom loved to play and did right up until the minute her hands turned complete traitor on her and she no longer could. She did her damnedest to teach all of us and pass down this love of music but at the time Betsy and David turned out to be her best students, Robin and I were too busy playing baseball and such to care. If I have any regrets in life, and I guess everyone has a few, that would be one of the biggest.

They both loved big band music. It was the music of the war and the soundtrack of a large portion of their lives. Benny Goodman, Glenn Miller, the Andrew sisters and the Maguire Sisters, Artie Shaw wove their way through a lifetime condensed into a half-dozen-years. The folks attempted to learn to dance but it was never their forte.

Everyone in the family had their own taste in music. Robin liked the fifties and Elvis and the Dave Clark Five, Betsy was Beatles and Stones, Hendrix and Cream, David and I seem to just float along with whatever was happening at the moment.

The beauty of that arraignment was no one really wanted to go hear what the other enjoyed, so when one or the other could scrape up the cash for a concert, and didn't want to go alone, they would take me!

Mom would dress me up, and later it would become David's turn, and take us to concert halls to hear Shostakovich, Beethoven and Mozart. Making certain we understood how important this music was.

Dad took a 14-year-old me and mom, I believe she went under protest, to hear some hillbilly singer down at Music Hall in Cleveland. We sat enthralled as this man came out and sang and told stories for a couple hours with just him, a bar stool, a guitar and a microphone. No band, no accompanists of any kind, just him and his songs, and the crowd was on the edges of their seats. You could hear people breathing as he sang. It was the most marvelous thing this kid had ever seen, and it made me want to do that. Though I would never be an Eddie Arnold. It was like sitting with a favorite uncle out on the front porch, swinging and rocking in the summer dusk, sipping lemonade and listening as he sang your life. Just life changing.

As my sister hit her teen years, and my dad was going out of town more often, they decided she needed a chaperone if she was going to date. What could be more in the way than a kid brother? Yes, I would accompany my sister and her beau, Vince, on their dates. As this usually involved going to hear him play with his band or going to hear one of his friends play I was all for it. And, then, getting to hang out with the band after the gig at Arby's while they talked about the music. It was heaven.

It also meant seeing some of the best concerts of the time. We saw the Beatles, Jimi Hendrix at Music Hall, Cream and dozens of other acts passing through Cleveland. Chaperone turned out to be the best job of all time. And it was the folks, my dad's in particular, idea. So, you can see where the blame for my life lays! Squarely at their feet. I rest my case, your honor.

After my high school career ended I did manage to get involved in a free clinic that had been set up in the Briardale Projects in Euclid. We helped folks with drug related problems, health, birth control and counseling. We worked with doctors and nurses, we had a good relationship with the police and the community. We were doing our best to help people.

One night they had a slight emergency with an overdose and

called me to come help. I was a manager at the time. As I drove, albeit a bit too fast, to help, I got pulled over. The cop didn't care for my excuse, I went to court, the judge, Niccum and a friend of my parents, didn't like my attitude and I didn't care for his, we had words, I lost, the usual outcome when arguing with any judge, and he decided I might be better off without my license for six months.

I stormed out of the courtroom, directly to my car and drove home. Obviously angry I stormed into the house announcing I was going to go to California. I had my last paycheck of $186 and a half tank of gas. My mother tried to talk me out of this course of action, I was not in the mood to be reasonable. She said just wait until your dad gets home and talk to him. I explained he was not going to be home until Friday and by then I would be sitting in San Francisco. As explained I could be a bit headstrong and unreasonable at this time, something I believe I inherited from my father!

By the time I got to friend's house in San Francisco, friends from Milwaukee who'd moved out to the west coast a year before, I was tired, broke and questioning my judgement. Not that I would tell my mother that. Then the generator went out on the mighty VW. I called home. Of course, the folks were there to catch me once again. My father might get pissed at you, he might wish to strangle you but when you came crawling back he was always the first to take you back in. Oh, he didn't forget. You got to live with your stupid for a while, that was the price. But he'd forgive. I think because he'd done some things in his life he knew had not been the brightest choices and he might have liked to change the past but knew he couldn't. The past is the only thing set in stone in life. You can change now and the future, but you can only learn from the past.

I believe that was the thing that infuriated him the most. He did everything in his power so we wouldn't do the same stupid things he did, make the same mistakes that made life harder for him. And when we didn't listen, when we did something stupid he was actually upset with himself for not having the wherewithal to stop us. It was as if our moronic behavior was a reflection on his failure to make us smarter by osmosis. I can't say for sure, but I know that's how I felt when my kids did something dumb. The car got fixed and I moved back as far as Milwaukee. Only to find out I missed them and Cleveland. I headed home to their welcome embrace. No matter how cold it might be, I knew it would warm with time. I had been gone just under a year. As I have said before, the folks were always there, always providing that safety net to catch you just before you crashed and burned, that allowed each of us to try our wings and find ourselves. That is one hell of a gift.

My father never judged, he would critique, he would make his displeasure known but at the end of the day he allowed us to live our own lives, dream our own dreams. My parents were not the sort of people who said, 'I love you'. I don't remember ever hearing those words from either of them, but I knew. They didn't shower you with praise and meaningless worship. They'd showed their love by always having your back, by encouraging with a word or two and letting you know when you were on the wrong road. They gave you the freedom to fail and the security to try. There is no better gift. They were there for support.

My folks were always completely immersed in their professional as well as private lives. My father was involved in charities and benevolent organizations since he returned from the war. Whether it was the American Legion, the VFW, Cub Scouts, Elks, Masons, whoever, if the organization was doing something to help other people he was in. But they also enjoyed sharing fun, laughter and a cocktail with friends. So, in the fall of 1970 they formed a cocktail group. What this entailed was a group of friends, limited by space and numbers of weeks, that would meet every other Friday at one or the others home. They would socialize from six until seven thirty and no later. The fare was to be simple, finger foods and a couple drinks and at seven thirty everybody had to leave. Simple. You could go somewhere else and have a drink or continue the conversation, but you could not stay at the host's home. Several years later they changed the time to six thirty to eight to give folks a bit of time to get home from work and wash up.

It was a great group of people starting off with the 236 bunch. Then adding Blakemore's, Audia's and Niccum's; yeah, that one, but we had become friends over the years and joked with each other about the courtroom scene! Many of the original cast has since passed on, life is, if nothing else, ever changing. But other couples joined not so much to replace them as to bring their own flavor to the stew. And to keep the party going. The amazing thing is these cocktail parties continue to this day, three separate groups now, almost fifty years later!

It saddens the heart to think of those who have passed, John Chapel, Adrian Hasse, Ed Thompson, Sam and Helen Audia, Jerry Tarrantino, Milt Thomas, Ed Blakemore, Gene Burke, Evan Beacham, Bill Perry, George Calvert and more. As the list grows it still brings tears of joy and a smile to just hear their names and remember the times shared. The widows and widowers continue along with the 'new' kids, Rowe's, Sherman's, Modica's, Kirchner's and so many more that have added their names and life to this original group. The physical space has increased between homes, so the drinks aren't as plentiful, driving as opposed to walking, but the company is still just as lively.

The folks always loved to entertain and the house at 1720 was perfect for that purpose. It wasn't huge or palatial, but it was comfortable and lent itself to conversation and interaction. Between the kitchen, where people just naturally gravitate, in any house, to the back room and the small backyard and pool.

One time they had people coming over for some event or other and discovered just prior to the festivities, a huge wasps nest down inside one of the wooden poles of the fence surrounding the pool. There was not time to run to the hardware and buy wasp and hornet spray, so dad told Robin to grab the gas can out of the garage. Robin ran and grabbed the can bringing it forthwith to dad, who poured it all over the post. Then threw a match on the gas. FIRE!

Robin grabbed the hose, luckily right near-by, and they sprayed and smothered the fire out before it could spread to the house. The post was, of course, the one nearest the back of the house, two feet away. Dad was always a man of action. Perhaps not the right action but action nonetheless.

Luckily during this time and with all the moves mom was still able to find a teaching position out in the Willoughby/Eastlake school district. She loved teaching and was one of the best because of that love, so it benefitted all to have her in the classroom.

One of my favorite stories about mom and teaching was, one year she had a young girl transfer into her class during the middle of the school year. The girl was quiet, shy but in an odd, almost, frightened way. As if she was afraid to get close to others or just didn't know how. And no matter how mom tried to draw her out remained closed off and aloof. She didn't make friends, wouldn't talk to anyone, kids or teachers, and mom began to fret for the girl. There was definitely something wrong with this child and mom was going to figure it out. Finally, she sat down with her and tried to get her to talk. It soon became obvious the girl just couldn't understand mom. She concentrated on every word coming out of mom's mouth but didn't seem to recognize any of them. She didn't speak English. Well, that might have been nice to know.

So, mom tried German, nothing. French? Nothing. Spanish? Nothing. Latin? Why not? Mom loved languages and spoke a half dozen. She might not have been fluent in all these languages, but she spoke enough to get her point across and be understood. But nothing. Finally, she was able to get the girl to speak in her own language, at least a few words, and, due to her linguistic background, determined it was one of the Romantic languages and could only be Italian. The child was Italian. So, mom, in her inevitable way, got herself to the library, took out several books on English to Italian and began to teach herself Italian. Very quickly the girl began to emerge from her shell. She picked up more English words and phrases as mom translated and mom picked up more Italian as the girl began to speak more and could gesture what some words meant. It was quite the symbiotic relationship. Mom never gave up on anybody, it was quite evident why she and dad were such a good pair.

Euclid was home, they had lived in four other towns by now but none of them fit like Euclid, and they were back. They made friends with Mike and Vi Kosmetos, Mike was to become the President of Euclid city council, and they began a Thursday night ritual of beer and peanuts at Ronny Sons tavern up on Chardon road. It was here they would become close to Nick and Karen Marino, a fellow trucker from Yellow Freight, and whom I went to school with. He later he became a councilman with Mike Kosmetos as the council president. It was becoming quite the tight knit group of concerned individuals. People who were just as invested in their community as mom and dad were. They were people who cared deeply for the place they lived and wanted to improve it. They sensed if they worked together they could have an effect. And they did.

Around this time, the folks decided to start making the yearly pilgrimage to Indianapolis in late May for the Indianapolis 500. Mom and dad just gravitated toward almost any sporting event and the Indy 500 is so much more than that. It is pageantry and party, fast cars and loud fast cars, and exciting to be a part of. To be right there and feel in your bones as these cars would race by at almost two hundred miles an hour. It definitely got the heart and blood pumping. They were addicted the first time they went.

I believe it started off with just the family, my brothers and such, I went once, and then friends glommed on and it became more of a yearly pilgrimage. The group included the Kosmetos' and Marino's as well as others on and off over the years. They would all leave Saturday morning of Memorial Day weekend and caravan as far as Daleville, Indiana, where they would spend the night. Dinner at DoLinski's, maybe a beer or two, then back to the motel, maybe another beverage or three and then bed. Up early Sunday to drive to the track, all day racing and back home. It was a grueling two days but if the race car drivers could do this, then so could the fans!

Within two years of the move to Euclid the company moved dad up the ladder once again but this time without making him leave Cleveland. He was now the Vice President of Spector Freight overseeing total road operations and distribution centers for the United States. With main distribution in Cleveland and Chicago. He was glad of the promotion but much happier about staying put. He wasn't sure he could pry mom out of Northeast Ohio again. And he didn't much cotton to the idea of being a bachelor at 50!

It was at this time that dad first dipped his toes into the political waters. I don't believe he ever had any desire to actually run for an office, he had met and knew too many politicians and came to the conclusion he could never be one. He couldn't promise somebody something knowing there was no way he could fulfill that promise. Politicians might actually, somewhere deep down in their hearts, believe they can do all they promise but dad never believed it. It got you elected and then it was up to you what to do with the office.

He enjoyed finding people he believed in, those who would use the power of their office to benefit the city and the people, not themselves, and working for them. He threw his weight and name behind Judge Niccum, Mayor Tony Sustarcic, Councilmen Kosmetos and Nick Marino, and Tony Guinta's run for Mayor. And later in life he helped George Voinovich get elected to Governor of Ohio. He and mom got to go to the Inauguration Ball. These were people he knew. These were also people he knew cared about the city and the state. They were not running for self-aggrandizement but because they believed they could make a difference for all the people.

Ed Blakemore was very involved in the Knights of Columbus, and a dear friend, so, of course, mom and dad became active, though not members, in their activities. They put together bus trips to Nashville, Cincinnati, Washington, Williamsburg, Frankenmuth and Baltimore. Fund raisers and benefits. Good times to raise money for those less fortunate; a win-win.

In July of 1975 I married Robin Stratton in my parent's backyard, out by the pool, and our reception was at the Knights. And in September of 1975 the first grandchild of Robert and Carol Zonneville entered the world. My daughter Kathryn was born in 1975 at Euclid General Hospital. The family would continue for another generation! And I was about to get a big whoopin' of responsibility upside the head! Nothing like children to make you stop and reassess your choices in life.

My Brother Robin, by this time, had spent a year at Ohio State University and come to the realization that college was not his forte. He had a penchant and a genius for automotive mechanics and he loved working on cars. To this day he is the best mechanic I have ever known, he pulled my fat out of the fire more times than I care to remember.

Everyone who knew him knew he was the guy to take your car. He knew more than most, was willing to admit when he didn't and would find what he didn't know and never charged more than a fair price. Also, never did anything that didn't need doing.

Betsy was making high grades and doing very well at the University of Wisconsin-Madison. She was born for college and took to it like a fish to water. She loved it and I believe if she could have spent her life as an academic she would have in a heartbeat.

David was about to wrap up high school at this point and would graduate in June of 1975.

But not all was positive accomplishments and sunshine and roses. Earlier in the decade 236th Street, very unexpectedly, lost dear friend, neighbor and footballer Adrian Hasse to a heart attack. The block was thrown into shock and mourned hard. And then Stan Biddle was transferred to Holland. 236th was slowly coming apart and it was time to move on.

They bought a two-story colonial on Buchanan Court in Mentor. An old chapter closes and new one begins.

Z

Carol Alliger 1944

Bob and Carol
The Lovebirds

The Wedding Party in the Bowery

Robin, Mom, Betsy, David, Dad, Kim

One Happy American Family!

David Kim Betsy Robin

The Ancients-Allen, Duane, Dad, Richard

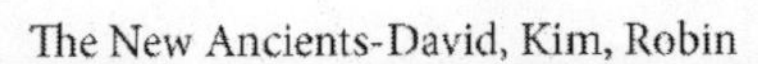

The New Ancients-David, Kim, Robin

Robin and Manette

Bob and Betsy

Cindy and David

Kim and Nancy

Greg, Jess,
Sam, Jackson, Madeleine

Berta, Vytas
Carolina, Augustas

Jack, CJ, Besty, Matt,
Isabella, Ellen, Bob, Madison

Robin, Manette, AJ, Jennifer, John

Adrienne

Katie and Jim

The Family!

Elvyra

Homes throughout the Years

Williamson

Tonawanda

Bear Swamp

1711 236th

Elm Grove

Brookfield

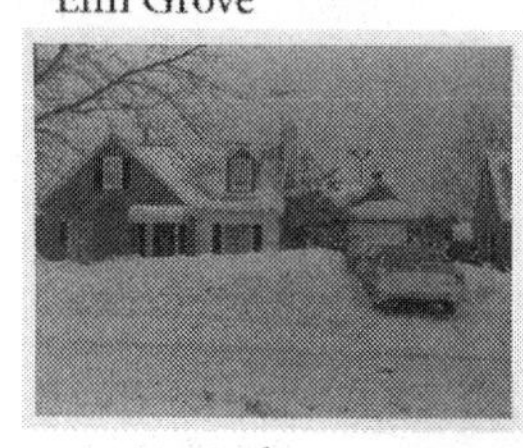
1720 236th

Mentor #1

Mentor #2

Florida/Alligers

Kathryn, Adrienne

Geiger/Kohn Fam

Elvyra, AJ, Manette

Mom, Dad
Grandma Ruthie, Grandpa

Uncle Ike Alliger

Grandpa Z

Greg, Jess, Kids, Grandfolks

Allen, Betty, Dana, Pete

Jon, Me, Jerica, Robert Black

Richard's Girls

Allen and
Betty

Duane and Virginia

Charlie, Donna and the Kids

Richard, Martha and the Family

Dana, Jerica, Steven, Jonathon, Deborah, Robert

Betty, Allen, Lori, Jeff

Combat Infantry Badge, ETO with 4 Bronze stars for Serving all 4 European Theaters, Bronze Star, Purple Heart, Good Conduct, Victory Medal, Occupation Medal, Medal awarded from the State of New York

The Legion of Honor
France's Highest Award

Mentor Days

It was 1978 and things were going well. They knew in their hearts it was time to leave the old neighborhood. Old neighbors had moved away, friends had passed, things change. It broke their hearts, but they also recognized it was time. 236 should be a neighborhood of young families starting out in life. These were homes affordable for those with young children wanting to buy in to the American dream. Homes that were close to schools, in safe neighborhoods. A place to begin building a life. Mom and dad were in the way. Time to move east and bucolic Mentor.

The house on Buchanan Court was huge compared to 236th Street. It became quite apparent that as each progressive child moved out the folks would buy bigger and bigger houses. Yeah, I know, but that was how they roll. Same number of bedrooms, living room, dining room and family room just bigger, including the pool. One thing they had discovered, buying Chapel's old house, was that they loved having a pool. It was the centerpiece for social gatherings. The kids, and now the grandkids, loved having a place to swim and play. The folks knew people would gravitate towards it in the beautiful Ohio summers. Even if someone didn't swim, there was something so relaxing about sitting around a pool on a warm summer evening with a cocktail and friends.

The new neighborhood in Mentor seemed like a perfect fit. Nice folks, quiet street, good neighborhood, the people were involved. But mom and dad weren't sure the new neighbors were ready for a

Zonneville invasion.

Once settled the folks invited the new neighbors over for a 'hello, get to know you' kind of event. Drinks and hors d'oeuvres, meet and greet, dip your toe in the new community, let them get to know the nice you before anything else can happen. It was a lovely evening and they truly were wonderful people. Fun loving, social, gregarious just like the folks. They all stayed until the end of the gathering, not late, but still a tiring evening of meeting, chatting with each and every neighbor, trying not to overlook anyone lest they feel marginalized; and be on your better behavior. They slept well knowing they could now relax into their new environs. Until the next day.

Apparently, the old gang decided not only did the folks deserve a nice send-off, after all there'd been a raucous going away soiree. Now they needed a fantastic, memorable welcome to their new home. So, the whole group of them caravanned out to the new neighborhood and parked out of sight; a street over. They gathered themselves up the street, around the bend where they could not be observed; though how you could miss the noise they made while assembling god only knows. But, when all was in place, the signal was given, and they had a dyslexic parade down Buchanan to the new Z House. They sang and danced and laughed and drank down the street. Bearers of food, drink and merriment. The new neighbors peering out their windows had to be wondering what insane fury hell had brought to their quiet, peaceful neighborhood.

The party lasted well into the night, some of the new neighbors just had to stop by to see what all the excitement was about, and immediately joined in. Exhausted after two nights of partying, the folks stayed indoors, worn out and 'tired' all day Sunday. They weren't sure if the new neighbors would be quite as welcoming Sunday as they had been on Friday. They had to be wondering what hurricane had hit them the night before, but all appeared quiet on the eastern front. They still smiled and waved at the new family, they didn't show scorn or displeasure, though I am sure this is not what they thought their new fifty something year old neighbors would be like. Adjustments would be made, and all would become great friends, once again.

My folks always seemed to meet the best people. They moved in the same circles and hung at the same joints, were involved in the same charitable organizations. But it was more than that. I remember as a kid hanging with my dad and my grandpa Alliger and being thoroughly convinced they knew every human being on the planet. Every cashier, server, dockworker, policeman, fireman, baker, bagger, beggar and thief. It didn't make any difference what someone did or where they worked these two seemed to know them. They would ask about their families or how the job was going. Sometimes it was just about the weather and the day. They knew, literally, everyone we ran across. They talked to everybody. Always with a smile, never long enough to irritate those in the line behind them but they always, always talked with whomever they ran across. How could they possibly know everybody?

After asking about this one day it was explained they didn't know any of these people. Oh, they had come to know some of them over the years, but they really didn't know them. They just knew they were people and deserved a 'hello' and 'how's your day going?', kind of thing. It was making a human connection. As my father explained to me one day, there are no strangers just folks he hadn't met yet. It didn't cost a nickel to be nice, to be decent, to care about someone else, it just took a minute. And everybody felt good in the long run. Besides, I believe dad and grandpa both just hated the silence of separation when standing so near another human being. They just didn't understand how you could be standing in a group of people, or next to someone, and not say something, a 'hello, how's your day?' it went against their nature. Yeah, you'd run into an ass or two along the way but everything in this world has a price.

About this time came the Lobster parties. Apparently when dad was still with Spector Red Ball one of the big muck-a-mucks came into town. He was a major stockholder and dad was to entertain him. As they talked over dinner the guy laughed and joked about how much my dad seemed to enjoy entertaining people. Why didn't he do more of it?

Dad mentioned he did a lot of it, customers, bosses, parties, whatever. What did he have in mind? Well, a friend of his was a lobster fisherman up near Boston and he could get dad a helluva deal on lobster's. Why not try lobster parties? You just throw them in a pot and boil them and people love it! And no one else, that he knew of, was doing anything remotely like lobster parties. Apparently, we were now a cocktail or two into the evening, but dad took to the idea.

So, dad tried one at the house for three or four of their better customers, ones he knew if it went awry he wouldn't lose them. He called the lobster man, dropped the muck-a-mucks name, and next day had a box of lobsters at the house. The prep was easy, the dinner was fun, delicious and a huge success.

Soon he was putting on lobster parties all over the Midwest as a way to drum up business and to raise money for this charity or that. He would set up meetings with prospective clients and afterward they would retire to wherever the kitchen had been set up and dad would cook lobsters. Lots and lots of lobsters. He'd, of course, made friends with the lobster fisherman from up around Boston who shipped live lobsters to wherever dad was going next. So, lobsters were flying from Boston to Saginaw, Paducah, Toledo, Detroit, Grand Rapids, Ft. Wayne, Rochester, Columbus, Indy, Rockford, IL and Milwaukee. A good portion of these folks had never seen a lobster let alone eaten one; one that had been alive just moments before. It was a good show and damn good eating.

These parties expanded out to included fundraisers for different organizations. I swear there was a time that lobsters came close to being an endangered species for all the parties dad threw for friends, business associates and to benefit others. One time he and mom, while staying at their condo in New Hampshire, decided to drive down to Boston for dinner. They got there early in the afternoon and dad suggested finding where this lobster fella was and visiting his business. They'd never met and dad had been buying lobsters from him for ten years. They found the business and walked in. The man working asks if he can help and dad asks if Paul Surrette is around. "Yes, he is and you are talking to him. You must be Bob Zonneville, I recognize your voice. You're my best customer, you've about decimated the lobster population all across the Atlantic seaboard." They got to tour the whole facility and visit for the afternoon. These two remained friends forever.

You will note throughout this narrative that steel thread; helping others. I don't know if it was because he had been helped by other students and teachers after being hit by the car or if was because of the kindness afford him during his time of war, the camaraderie of battle and being there for each other. But I don't think a day has passed in my father's life that he wasn't doing something, large or small, to help another human being. Besides, I think dad was a born entertainer. He loved to put on the show, but mostly, he loved to see people happy.

In the fall of 1978, well settled in the new neighborhood and all getting used to each other, they began another cocktail group. They would meet once a month but for the same time, an hour and half. The idea was not so much a party but to keep everyone connected no matter how busy their everyday schedules would become. You knew once a month you took that hour and a half to reconnect with neighbors and the activities of the street and community. It was a great way for all to be involved with the area and town. Neighborhoods are safer, healthier and more a village when everyone is connected. A smile, a wave as you walk down the street, just a quick human connection is sometimes all it takes.

They started off with six couples and within the year had expanded to twelve so as to have a house for each month. A burden shared is a burden no more with a couple cocktails. It was a great place to meet up and discuss neighborhood association projects and plan new ones, such a clam bakes, picnics for the families, golf outings, casino nights, safer streets and upkeep. They even built a float for the annual Better in Mentor Days Parade. All in all, a very involved and great group of people.

Things were humming along on the professional front as well. Dad was now Vice President of Spector Red Ball and Mom was building tenure teaching in Willoughby/Eastlake school district. They we finally doing well financially, and both were very happy in their professions, their friends and, especially, their private lives.

My parents were not the kind of people who openly displayed affection. They were not huggee, kissy kind of folks. They didn't unnecessarily throw around I love you's. As a matter of fact, I don't remember ever hearing those words from either pair of lips. But they proved it everyday of their lives. They didn't say it, but a touch of the hand, a hug, a look, how comfortable they were with the other near, showed more love than words. Tenderness is not found just in words, romance can be sparked by time. The passion one has for each other does not burn brilliantly every moment of your lives. Sometimes it is banked and left smoldering, the embers warm, like a down comforter, ready to be stoked. Love is a series of hills and valleys, you just got to enjoy the view as you go!

Life is fluid if nothing else. 1982 came and things changed hard. Spector filed bankruptcy and was closing down. Dad was 57 years old and looking down the loaded barrel of unemployment. As he was an officer in the company they asked if he could stay on a few weeks to help dispose of freight and furniture. Of course he would, he had no other options. He received a reprieve on June 9th of '82 when they said they would transfer him over to Viking Freight, one of the divisions of Spector that would continue. He could keep the paycheck coming and the wolves from the door! Then, on July 1st they announced they were closing Viking. But they were trying to find some way to keep him employed. He said, thanks but no thanks, he'd had enough of the roller coaster ride and he wanted off.

Before closing, the last folks standing and in charge of what was left of a major trucking company, informed dad that there was an investor group wanting to start up a new trucking concern from the bottom and they wanted to talk to him. If he would, they wished to meet with him at the Chicago O'Hare Motel as soon as he could arrange it. Well, of course, he would, he had no other options at this point. He met them within a few days and they told him if he would join forces with them they would add him to the payroll on July 10th. His final payday from Viking was July 9. Sometimes it pays to be lucky, sometimes being lucky is predicated on being good and people knowing it.

On July 11th Independent Freightway was officially open for business, though it would quickly become known as Inway. He didn't want to move again so accepted a demotion to Regional Manager and a cut in pay, so he and mom could stay in Mentor. The last thing my mother wanted was another move, another disruption in life. She certainly didn't want to go job hunting for another teaching position at her age. School systems were seeking young, just out of college teachers, teachers they could pay substantially less than they had to pay one of my mom's experience and years teaching. And the last thing in the world my father wanted was to upset the woman he loved. His territory was now Ohio, Michigan, Eastern Indiana, western Michigan and Western New York. He set up his office on West 65th Street in Cleveland. The company was officially underway.

It was more than underway, it was growing like a raging fire. And through hard work and perseverance they continued to throw more combustibles on the inferno. At the end of the first year Inway gave my father half of what he'd lost in his cut in salary. He was now receiving awards and commendations. The new president of the new company, Jeff Crowe, was a dynamic individual who knew how to make people excited about their work and want to give their all. He, in turn, was a great person to work for who inspired and was not afraid to take chances and go out on thin limbs. Success comes not from safely watching others but in the risk of doing. Of course, you need to plan well, research your concepts and execute, but you have to be willing to try. He encouraged all, plus they knew he had an extensive background in trucking; he knew of which he spoke. My father always spoke very highly of this man and often wondered where the company would have wound up had there been another in charge.

One of the fun ways he would inspire folks to give their all is start-up annual conventions for all agents who did a million dollars in revenue, a quite attainable goal. Inway was a consortium of independent truckers, and agents who found them loads to carry, all under one banner. The agents would sell customers on shipping with 'Inway' and the company did the logistics of matching up truck with load.

The conventions were a way to show the agents they appreciated their efforts all year round, plus they were to bring their wives. A lovely couple day getaway, all paid for by Inway. The very first convention was held on a Caribbean cruise. They ate, they drank, they mingled and got to know each other better. One thing about becoming closer personally it makes the competition more delectable professionally. Nothing like a little one on one friendly competition with a buddy to see who can have the highest numbers year to year. All had the time of their lives and were motivated to return the next year. Each year they found a new and exotic locale that tantalized and motivated each agent to achieve.

They held management meetings at Eagle Ridge Golf Resort in Galena, Illinois, a beautiful course in the rolling hills of northwestern Illinois. These would create memories and camaraderie as well as friendly competition between the regions. You would come for a weekend of meetings and setting the years goals and leave charged up and ready to take on the world. Jeff was an excellent leader.

When the company began in 1982 my dad told mom that he believed the company was capable of doing over fifty million dollars a year in revenue; they quickly raced by that marker. He was having a ball. Sometimes you need a swift kick to re-engage your love of job. Dad, without knowing it, had needed the challenge that this start-up company had provided. He felt like a kid again and was enjoying his work more than he had in years.

During this period of growth and change from the mid-seventies through the mid-eighties the family was growing and moving about. My wife and I had our second child, Adrienne, in 1977. My brother David got married in 1978 and moved across the street from where we lived on 152nd Street. Grandpa Alliger passed in 1974 and Grandpa Zonneville in 1978. It is the constant expansion and contraction of family.

Betsy married Bob Schulz in 1976 and they remained in Madison where they began their family 1979 with the birth of Ellen. We were uncles and aunts for the first time on the Zonneville side. Gregory would later join the Zonneschulz family in 1981. Robin was building his business after taking over Tony and Paul's gas station at 222nd and Euclid. He later married Manette Reebel in 1985 bringing along the marvelous and lovely Jennifer, born in 1980, a new niece to love. David and Clarisa parted ways in 1984 and he finally met and married Cindy in 1995. A small time of upheaval and settling once again. But all in all, the family was thrumming along.

I had become divorced from Robin, irreconcilable differences, and had the greatest of good fortune to meet, fall deeply in love with, court, win the love of and be allowed to spend the rest of my life with Nancy Mumford. This ranks as the smartest thing I had ever done in my life, though Ms. Mumford might question her own wisdom in taking on the project.

Mom and dad were pleased as the extended family grew and prospered but a little sad as the nucleus shrank. They were now down to just the two of them and the dog. There was always a dog. From time immemorial there would always be dogs. Punky led to Pandora to Sheila of Sherwood, the only dog we ever had with official papers and a title, Heidi, Arica, Schultzie, Bailey, all the way to Angel. Dogs rule the Zonneville family tree. Every dog was a German Shepherd, well, Pandora was a Shepherd/Doberman mix, but the rest were Shepherds. All were loved, all were more than spoiled, all could be a huge pain in the ass and all were mourned, grieved and wept over when they passed. They were family and we really don't care what your opinion of that might be; so, shut it.

All the dogs were big, intimidating and quite lovable. Pandora had an attitude, but she'd earned it. When we lived at 168 DeKalb, she was quite young and energetic. If someone came to the door, she barked. It was her job. And she loved her job and was good at it. One time the mailman in full mailman regalia come to the door, knocked and was greeted by the barking, snarling large, Shepherd/Doberman dog. The dog jumped on the screen door, catching the handle and it opened enough for her to stick her head out. He freaked and whacked her across the nose with his mailman chain. It left a scar she would carry for life. From that day on she HATED anyone in a uniform.

One day, unbeknownst to anyone, she got out of the yard. We didn't know how long she was gone nor where she had wandered, we just knew when she returned at a quick pace she had a large swatch of blue cloth between her teeth. Mom heard her scratching at the door, let her in, spied the blue hanging from her mouth and threw her down into the basement.

Just in time as there was now a loud banging on the same door. She smoothed her clothes and, calmly, went to the door to confront the very angry postal worker standing on the stoop.

“Do you know anyone around here with a big, black dog?” he demanded.

“Why no, I don’t believe I do,” she oozed innocence, ignoring the barking and snarling coming from behind the basement door.

“Well, when I find it I am going to shoot the bastard! It bit my ass and tore my new pants!” he screamed.

“Well, good luck,” said mother sweetly as she closed the door.

In all fairness to my mother, who would never lie, Pandora was not black. She was mostly black with brown markings. He should have been more accurate in his description. Mom was always a stickler for accuracy. The folks had to pick up their mail from the post office for a bout a year as no mailman would again come to the house. David swears this also played out another time but with a cop, though same piece of cloth in same dog’s jaws. She hated uniforms!

When uncle Al came home from Korea, after being discharged, he showed up at the door proudly decked out in uniform. Pandora went nuts and chased him around the house until the folks could corral her and then lock her in the basement. It was the last time Allen showed up in uniform.

The folks also began a lifelong love of international travel. My mother swore she would never travel beyond the US/Canadian borders and hung pretty tight to that vow. With the slight exception of a hellish trip to Bermuda in 1968. Yeah, I know, right? Hellish trip to Bermuda?

Here is a brief synopsis of the trip. We are to fly from Milwaukee to Bermuda for a once in a lifetime holiday. The day of the departure a snowstorm of catastrophic proportions hits the Midwest. We are socked in and can’t take off. I probably should mention at this point that my mother is not the best flyer in the history of mankind, it made her nervous, to be kind. The luggage has been checked and promises are made that it will be held until the next day and put on the plane with us, we are headed home for a good night's sleep and to try again in the morning. The storm abates long enough for us to get in the air, after a bumpy take-off, and are now flying the friendly skies and free.

We travel casual. I know at the time this is verboten, it is the 60's and people still dress up to fly. It is a special treat, they still have actual china and silverware on these flights, and not to be trifled with by a bunch of hooligans in sweat shirts and jeans. But it is also the end of the 60's and we like to be comfortable, especially when we are going to be in the air for four or five hours. So, we get to Bermuda and a beautiful, expensive, hotel. Everything is magnificent except there is no luggage. We are in the clothes we flew in. Not to worry, they will be here tomorrow, assures the airlines. So, dad buys us some shorts and shirts and such, beachwear, so we can explore Bermuda.

The next day dawns and it's another no show on the clothes. It's OK, mon, we got beachwear, it's warm, there is sand and surf and we're just fine, thank you very much. We continue our touring, Bermuda is a beautiful, lush island, catering to the neer-do-wells and wealthy. Dad rents a couple scooters, if memory serves and we are seeing the sites.

Along about sundown we need some dinner. Dad hails a cab and explains we would like to find someplace where we can find island type food for dinner. I don't know if the cabby misunderstood, didn't look at who he was hauling or thought it was funny, but he took us to a local joint he knows and swears by the food. Our day out now includes an evening stop in what turns out to be a nativist, island kind of almost strip club. Oh, there's calypso music and tiki torches and lots of bamboo, but they seem to feature scantily clad women dancers. Here come mom and dad schlepping into this joint with four kids in tow. We haven't eaten and we're hungry. We're staying. As the evening progresses Mom is becoming very uncomfortable, dad doesn't care there is food, and it is quite tasty, and beer, most of us think it is just part of the show. You know, different cultures, different mores. Fire eaters, limbo, dancing, sparsely clad women and mom turning red. She is demanding we leave, now dragging us by the hand, ear, whatever she can grab, and we are now waiting outside as dad pays the check. A delightful evening.

Why didn't you just eat at the fancy hotel you are staying at, you ask? Well, we couldn't eat at the fine restaurant in the hotel because you needed a suit coat and tie to be seated. It was a bit upscale and we didn't give that impression in our beachwear. Our suit coats as well as pants, shirts, underwear and socks were somewhere in flight. Finally, my dad has had enough. The third night he marches up to the maître d' and announces that the hillbillies will be seated in their fine restaurant as we are paying a fortune to be there. They can either find us jackets and ties or seat us as we are. They found suit jackets of varying sizes and ties of some sort, for us to slip on over our floral shirts and shorts.

At this point, one would think they would find a nice quiet corner to tuck us away in, where none of the other well-bred, finely tailored guests would notice us or have their meals spoiled by dining with the Clampetts. Nope. Right smack dab in the middle of restaurant. We didn't care at this point, stare, scowl, point, we were going to eat. The service was excellent, quick and attentive. 4 stars.

This was another nail in the coffin, albeit more of a spike, of mom ever having any desire to travel outside the good ol' USA. Then, Holiday Inn, to show their gratitude, rewarded my father for his loyalty of always staying in their hotels wherever he would travel, and remember he traveled a lot, with a two week, all expenses paid, vacation to London, England. It took a great effort and months of convincing but he finally, by hook or by crook, got mom to agree.

They spent Christmas and New Year's 1982 hobnobbing around jolly old and, especially, London, and they had the most wonderful time. Mom loved the history of London and the architecture, the stories, the bobbies, the cabs, everything and fell in love with the idea of seeing the rest of the world. I remember her going on about the age of the country. You could feel it weighing on you, the centuries of civilization. Our country is a very young country. Just over two hundred years. These people have been drinking in pubs that were two hundred years old when we were in our infancy. Great Britain is a nation that has existed for more than a thousand years. The castles still stand centuries since they were built. London was this puzzle of humanity constructed over two thousand years. It was mindboggling, and she wanted more.

I believe Ireland was next in 1983. They joined a group excursion led by Bob Murphy, who wrote for the News Herald paper out in Lake county, and his wife Ann. Naturally, they became fast friends and traveled together for many years. Dad also found, in Murphy, another person involved in helping others, so they worked on golf outings, to raise money for hospice, as well as other causes. What could be better than to share a round of golf, a couple of beers, all for the benefit of someone else. We're drinking for the kids here! Anyway, the parents so loved the Emerald Isle they returned another seven times. They were smitten with seeing, experiencing, submersing themselves in other cultures, older civilizations and the beauty of the rest of the world. They would travel until it became impossible, physically, to do so.

They also were feeling pretty flush financially and, considering where they had come from, how low at points of life they had sunk, you can see where, in their minds, they believed it to be true. They were better off than they had ever been in life. And that life seemed to have stabilized.

Inway was chugging along, mom was well placed in the Willoughby/Eastlake school district, so they purchased some time sharing. A way to invest in vacation time in areas they loved to visit here in America. You bought weeks at a resort, for few thousand dollars per, and then when your week came up it was a couple hundred dollars maintenance fee and you were basking in the sunshine and warmth of a beach town for an entire week. It actually was a pretty good deal because if you couldn't use your week, or wanted to go anywhere they had resorts, you could 'space bank' your time and use it elsewhere.

The first purchase they made was finding a pretty good deal on four weeks in Myrtle Beach. A couple years later they were traveling up through New England and enjoyed it so much they purchased another week in New Hampshire. They could jump from there to Boston of a day trip or drive up through the mountains of New Hampshire, Vermont and Maine. Something they loved to do, just get in the car and see where the road less traveled would lead.

Between all the weeks it provided plenty of time and space for all in the family to vacation when finances would allow. Everyone used the time shares at one time or another. Quite the deal. They bought the time and we just had to pay a maintenance cost if we wanted to use one of the weeks. It made it very affordable for any us to take our kids on a vacation they, or we, would never have gotten.

Out of the blue, Willoughby/Eastlake school district came to mom in 1985 with the offer of a buyout. The school system would pay her to retire early. She would get full bennies now rather than wait another half dozen years. The bean counters in administration had discovered over the years it was cheaper to buyout those with the most experience, therefore with the highest salaries, and hire younger, less experienced, read: cheaper, teachers. Mom could get full retirement with only thirty-one years credit. It would include a nice pension as well, they could hardly refuse, so mom retired. And my father dreamed of luxurious retirement down the road. I kid, my father never dreamed of retirement in his life as he was having far too much fun with his job. When you love something, why would you walk away, especially when they are willing to give you money to do something you would do for free? Forget that last sentence!

By 1989 Inway had consolidated with Ranger, Ligon and Gemini and was now headquartered in Shelton, Connecticut. The head of this company might have been a businessman of some sort, but that sort was not trucking. He had neither the head nor experience for trucking and really didn't care to learn. Business was business and you run one like any other. This would be wrong.

Finally, the group decided their wisest course of action would be to bring Jeff Crowe up the corporate ladder fast enough to knock the other fella out. They were absolutely correct. Jeff was the perfect person to start Inway and he would be used to his full potential as CEO of the entire corporation. He was smart, savvy in trucking and people liked and respected him.

This meant the position of President and CEO of Inway was open. They offered it to my father, initially he refused. He had made the promise not to uproot my mother again and he took his promises to heart. They were now in their sixties and no one was in the mood for another move. But a discussion happened one night as they sat after dinner enjoying an after-dinner drink.

As the discussion progressed my mother said to him, 'You started off with nothing but poverty and hardship on the Bear Swamp road, served in the war, wounded twice, screwed around for a couple years until you found trucking. You drove trucks, loaded trucks and have done everything in this business, YOU LOVE THIS BUSINESS AND THIS COMPANY, it would be wrong not to end that career as the president of this company.' As my mother was now retired, and, apparently, insistent, he accepted the position, much to everyone's pleasure, and they moved to Rockford, Illinois.

Once again goodbyes were hard, as they had become quite woven into the Mentor community as well as an integral part of the neighborhood. But dad had to consider my mother's point, forty years before he was driving truck and loading trucks on the dock, a hard, hot, cold, miserable way to make a living. He'd used his personality, intelligence, willingness to learn and his belief in himself to become a dispatcher, regional dispatcher, assistant terminal manager, manager, regional manager and Vice president, how could he possibly refuse to listen to my mother and not cap off this career as President and CEO? Of course, the extra pay and benefits wouldn't hurt either.

And as a bonus, Robin and Manette would be buying the folks house on Buchannan. They had always loved the house, the pool, the yard and the location. They already knew all the neighbors from coming to parties at the house over the years, so it was the perfect solution. Plus, mom could stay there for a bit while dad found a house for them in Rockford.

And The Beat Goes On

So, early in 1989 he became the president and CEO of Landstar INWAY and the folks continued their Gypsy ways and moved to Rockford, Illinois. Inway continued its growth under my father's direction increasing revenue from $130 million dollars his first year to more than $150 million dollars when he retired three years later. He just had to continue the programs and incentives Jeff Crowe and he had instituted since the inception of the company.

Oh yeah, the 'retirement'. After his first year as Prez and CEO they had their annual convention in Monterey, California. It was spring, business had been very good, the flowers were blooming, and all had one helluva time. It must have been one of the best conventions ever as people still talk about it to this day.

After the convention concluded the head of Landstar set up for some of the top grossing managers and sales people to play a round of golf at Pebble Beach. For those unfamiliar with Pebble Beach it is one of the great Mecca's of golf. It is the number 1 public golf course in the country. They've hosted five U. S. Opens with the sixth coming in 2019, five U.S. Amateur's and a PGA tour event every year since 1947. It is one of the most beautiful spots on earth to play golf, extremely challenging and something to boast about to anyone who cares to listen and many who don't.

My father explained during this time his desire to retire in 1992.

He would have the three-year, top of the company, feather in his cap. And the distinction of ending his career at the top of his game, and as President and CEO of a major corporation. Not bad for the son of poor, dumb Dutch immigrants who faced poverty and loss most of their early lives. He would be 67 and it would be time to hang up the cleats.

Landstar would have nothing to do with this insanity. Yes, he could retire as the top man in the company, but they wanted him to stay on for a bit as a consultant for special projects and inspiration. They also agreed to move he and mom back to Mentor. What can a poor boy say? He agreed to stay on for a little while.

Then again, in 2005 he explained, no, he really meant it this time, he had to be moving on. It had been fun and all, but it was time to retire, no, he meant it. He'd spent the last thirteen years visiting other companies, the larger accounts, as an ambassador of good will and sales. Doing extra glad handing and cooking lobsters and creating new business in general. He also spent time in Jacksonville, Florida, helping to train people in their new logistics division. It had been a very busy part time job, though as payment for him sticking around Inway had paid for his season tickets to the Indians, Browns and Cavs. He just had to use a certain amount for business; deal. Once again, we the people benefitted from dad's hard work and diligence as we were allowed to scarf up the available tickets for the rest of the games. This was during the mid-90's and the Indians were on a tear, tickets were hard to come by and we each bought our fill of some of the best seats in the house. It was a joyful time for the baseball loving Zonnevilles!

During his time earlier with Spector and throughout his time with INWAY he'd built a reputation for the lobster parties. By the end of his tenure he had put on parties in, but not limited to, Buffalo, Rochester, Grand Rapids, Rockford, Milwaukee, Fort Wayne, Columbus, Louisville, one in Paducah, KY for 50 people, one in Toledo for 60 and the largest in Detroit for over 200 people. There was no one who could carry the torch from here. This was a ton of work with dad being the head cook and bottle washer for these events. He was a trucker not a chef, but he managed, because he truly enjoyed putting the parties on. As I said he was quite the entertainer. It was impressive, and he used his powers not just for business but also for good to raise money for charities.

But it was time. He knew this because many events over the past decade had convinced him it was time to hang up the work shoes for what time he had with his family.

I believe one, or really two, of those events were my daughter, Adrienne's bouts with cancer. In 1990 she was diagnosed with stage two Hodgkin's Lymphoma. The family had gathered at Southwest Hospital in Cleveland as she had gone in for a minor operation on a lump in her neck. The doctor told us what he thought, cancer, stage two, and we sat stunned for a few moments. All of us, quiet. My wife Nancy, her folks, Earl and Ruth, two of the finest people I was lucky enough to have fall into my life when they allowed me to marry their daughter, my ex-wife and her husband Tom, daughter Katie, and my mom and dad, all afraid to utter a word. Really, not knowing what to say. What can you say?

"What are you going to do?" Asked my father, steady as a rock.

"Take it one step at a time and beat it." Said I with much more confidence that I felt.

She became the youngest person ever to have a port implanted in her arm. The port is an artificial vein to inject chemo that goes right to the heart. The concept being that giving all these chemicals into an organic vein would destroy it. This was the best solution for all.

They didn't want to hit her with radiation as she was so young and still growing and the radiation could very well stunt her growth. So, it was chemo and puking, outpatient care, six to eight hours of therapy and then three or four days of throwing up on the couch at home while we played the asses and forced food in her. You have to eat, or you die. Dying was not an option. So, my wife and I lived with the guilt of forcing her to swallow mashed up food and liquids while she glared her hatred our way.

We, like my folks before me, had no health insurance, we would pay as we went. One time I got a call from my wife, who had just been to the pharmacy, weeping, explaining how the prescription she'd just picked up was over four hundred dollars. And we would have to do this twice a month for the next six months! And it was only one prescription! What would we do?

The same as the folks and the grand folks had done before them, make promises, make payments, make good. We made a deal with Doctor Shurin, she would keep Adrienne alive, we would pay the bill. It might take a bit of time, but we would pay it.

I had learned from my father if you are upfront and honest with people they will work with you and trust you. They did. The hospital helped find some funding and adjusted what they could on the bills. Dr. Shurin did as well. She was a Godsend and inspiration. As were my folks and Nancy's. All chipped in with time, cooking, cleaning, helping. Family, pain in the ass family, what would you do without them?

It took less than a year and she was pronounced cancer free. Hallelujah. We could now move on with our lives.

In 1994 she was diagnosed with stage four Hodgkin's Lymphoma. They started talking percentages of survival. If I have learned nothing else from my father, it is to believe. Don't tell me percentages tell me what we have to do to beat this again.

Once again, we were all sitting together at University when the news came. I excused myself, went to the bathroom and wept, silently, so no one would hear and came out to face my family. My father is the rock, he is the strength I draw from and was on that day more than at any time he has pulled my bacon from the fire.

Adrienne has always said how much strength she took from me that day. She knew I had lost it in the bathroom but when I came out I just asked what was needed for us to do. What did they need from our family. I don't think she ever knew how much I drew from my father that day.

This time there would be radiation as well as chemo, they would hit her hard and we would beat it again. They probably mentioned at some point what these poisons were doing to her body and I probably blew off the info, just save her life. The family was, once again there, helping. Our dear friends, like Barb Sandon, dropping off a dinner just when it was needed and Sue North coming over, letting herself in while Nancy was at the hospital, and cooking dinner so my wife wouldn't have to.

That is the thing about going through something like this. It is the little things, the guy who stops by to cut the grass, so you don't have to, the friend who drops off a meal so you, tired and drained from mental and physical exhaustion, can just unwrap, heat and eat. The phone call to ask how you are and mean it. My father had warned me, explained how this would go, "you will discover who your true friends are. You will find out who really cares and who you can count on." He knew. He'd seen it, lived it and remembered who had shown up when he was laid up for all those months after the accident and when his appendix burst. And he was, as usual, right.

Dad would call from the road to see how my wife and I were doing. He didn't offer money, he didn't have to, I knew, I knew deep in my bones, if I needed it, it would be there. I didn't want to need it. Luckily, and there is that word again, I was making more money that I ever had in my life. It might take every nickel, but we would pay our bills.

Friends, one time, worked with my wife, mom and dad to set up a fundraiser for us. They didn't say anything to me until it was too late for me to cancel it. They raised $13,000. My dad glowed the whole time. He said to me at one point, "you are a very lucky man." I looked at him, 'damn straight,' I thought.

My father has always traveled, from the time he and Uncle Duane ran routes with their father in the 1930's, and he had continued during his 'retirement'. It was time to stay home with mom. She needed him though wouldn't say it, but he knew, and it was time to give his girl all the time he could. Though the rest of the family doubted this was to be true. Well, the staying at home part.

For those who believed Bob Zonneville would rest on his laurels and lay back, all I can say is, you haven't been paying attention.

During the previous thirteen years they had continued their love of travel. As I mentioned earlier, they had met and joined forces with Bob and Ann Murphy and discovered the two of them were a hoot to travel with. Bob would put these trips together and then write about them for the News Herald. Really just a way to travel and see the world while pretending you were working and writing the whole thing off as a business expense; I think my dad loved that about Murphy more than anything else!

At one point Bob was planning a trip to Germany, Austria, Switzerland and Italy and mom and dad decided to glom on and see some more of Europe. But the folks decided they wanted just a wee bit more. So, they flew out a week early to Brussels where they rented a car to head towards Brugge and on to Schoondijke, Holland; his father's hometown. He had seen it during the war but now wanted to explore it just a bit, to walk around, feel the town without dodging Nazi's and gunfire. And that was about all he would get, as it is a tiny little place, a short tour with my mother.

Then they spent time driving around Holland, Luxemburg and then on to Frankfort, Germany to meet up with the rest of the tour. As much as the folks always enjoyed these planned tours, with up to thirty or so people-some of whom they had gotten to know and become tight friends with over the years and the time traveling together-though the group was fluid with people coming and going as time, finances and life would permit-I believe they enjoyed trips with just the two of them as much if not more. There is a freedom in traveling small with someone you love and like, experiencing things on a more personal level. No schedule, no agenda, no place they HAD to be. No, too much time here, that's enough there, why are we still here? and 'is it four o'clock and we haven't eaten lunch yet?' kind of touring. Sharing the beauty of a country, screwing up the language and laughing your way through a poorly ordered dinner-a quick aside, a famous story of my mother attempting to use very rusty French and ordering a hot dog with chips instead of the wonderful French entre she thought she was ordering-and just being two people enjoying each other's company.

For their 50th anniversary they needed to do something outstanding! 50 years together? You betcha! So, they went to France where they spent several days on a hotel barge touring wine country. They crept along the canals of rural French wine growing country, enjoying the food, wine and slow pace afforded by this relaxed form of travel until they reach the Seine and then headed back to Paris. Along the way my father found a spot near where they had docked for the night to take a hot air balloon ride high above wine country. You could see for miles as the whole of France was laid out before him. My mother, feet firmly planted on the solid earth, took his word for it.

Once back in Paris they spent several days taking in the sights and ordering the wrong food before hopping a bus to Omaha Beach and the Normandy American Cemetery. It was the first time since 1944 that dad had set foot on that beach. The Cemetery was almost more than they could bear. Gratitude for those who gave all and thankful he had been allowed to continue his life. There but for the grace of God...

The years passed, and the travel continued, they wanted to see and experience all they could out of life. As I may have mentioned, my folks never really made a whole lot of money, and they earned every nickel they did- both working their whole lives- but they spent as if they had a fortune. And they did; just not in capital. Apparently, my mother never really knew what all these trips cost and dad was not in the habit of informing her of things that would only put a damper on the trip. He would find a way to pay for them, he wanted her to be happy. That seems to have been his true life's work, making my mother happy. As they had come from completely different backgrounds, my father poor and digging in the dirt, my mother from some money and maids. He did all he could to bring her joy in thanks for marrying this poor, dumb dirt famer. As we say he didn't spoil her he inherited her that way.

Not to say she didn't know want or hunger, hard work and sacrifice. As a matter of fact, maybe she knew more than any of us, as she had come from such a wealthy background and then turned her back on all that could have been hers, to marry this man with nothing but promise. She had given up her privilege and comfort and picked cherries and apples by his side until her hands were blistered and sore. She had lived in poverty because of love. She stood by his side while he worked his way up the American ladder. They were equals in all they did, side by side, through good times and harsh, hard down times. Is it harder for someone who has never known this kind of life or for the guy who grew up that way and has never known what easy street must feel like? She must have loved him more than any of us can imagine.

They returned to England and Ireland several more times over the years and visited Iceland, Denmark, Norway, Sweden and Finland. Where once my mother swore she would never travel beyond the borders of the USA or Canada, we all considered Canada as an extension of us as we had grown up across the river, she now traveled to far off lands and experienced more than she could have hoped for. I still find it so bizarre that I need a passport to visit a country, Canada, we used to go to as easily as going to another town, city or state. Life changes.

She thought everything she would ever care to see, or experience, lay within the North American borders. She discovered over the years that though there was so much to be seen and loved within those confines there was so much more to unearth in the world. She had loved learning her entire life, there was no need to ever stop.

The folks sometimes didn't care if the travel made sense or was what others would do. There was the trip to Florida sometime in the mid 90's. They decided to fly to Key Largo, where the Kirchner's, Bill and Ellie, had relocated a few years before, for a weekend Super Bowl party. A bit of a trek for a party but they were not your normal people and they loved to surprise friends. OK, maybe they were a bit on the crazy side as well.

Throughout all this and into dad's actual retirement he did consulting work for different folks. I would guess his favorite was All Pro Freight. He and Chris Haas had become fast friends over the years and truly enjoyed collaborating on projects for years, though Chris was half his age. The two were like peas in a pod. They shared a love of trucking and sports, especially baseball. They have remained friends throughout the years even though they no longer share their working relationship.

He knew it was time to call his working life/consulting life quits as mom began to fade. Her memory was not what it had once been, and she was having trouble concentrating. There were still flashes of the old brilliant woman we all knew but they were becoming less and less frequent. Dad gladly gave up the work he loved so much for the woman he loved more.

Mom passed on August 11, 2008. She was interred in Arlington

National Cemetery on September 25, 2008. She had served as a WAVE during World War II in Washington D. C. as an Oceanic Cartographer. Which we always thought was hysterical as she really couldn't read maps. But in the time of war we all serve.

I look at that date and if fills my heart with sorrow, as I know it will all her children and grandchildren, her friends and former teachers and students. There is a hole in the world where my mother used to live. I know this is a book about my father and his life, but he wouldn't be my father nor had this life without my mother. They were as matched as any two people can be. It was their differences as much as their similarities that made them one.

I miss my mother's sense of humor. Her intelligence. My father has always said she was the smartest person he ever knew but I think he underestimates himself. He may not have had the school learning mom did, but he had the life learning she'd not had. She encouraged his love of book learning, his thirst for raw knowledge, and he encouraged her learning through experience, through life, what we call street smarts. They fed off each other in such a good way, sometimes it was hard to tell where one stopped and the other started.

For Christmas one year, my wife and I found mom a sweatshirt, yes, a sweatshirt, with a saying on it I thought mom would think hysterical. She opened the present Christmas morning and stared at this grey sweatshirt for a moment.

I said, "do you want to know what it says?" We giggled.

"I know what it says," she retorted feigning offense and outrage, "it says," in Latin, "if you can read this, you are over educated!" she laughed and put it on. Wore it the whole day.

Mom never showboated her intelligence, yet she saw no reason to hide it either. She would no more play dumb to make someone feel smarter than she would feign hunger to make someone feel full. It was not in her make-up. She would no more belittle herself than she would belittle another. If you don't wish to appear as stupid or uneducated then do not be stupid or uneducated.

Read!

Man, if there is one word that defines both Bob and Carol

Zonneville, that is it! They both were voracious readers. There were always books on tables, in bookshelves, next to beds. Granted they couldn't read as much as they liked when they were younger and working two jobs and raising a family-sometimes life gets in the way of the things we enjoy- but they always managed to find some time for books.

They read to us as children and encouraged us to read on our own. You were never alone, never bored, never idle if you had a book in your hands. It is probably a generational thing, like x-box or something, but I feel sorry for those who don't take the time to read something, anything, just open the theater in the mind, sit back and enjoy.

They read mostly biographies and the classics, Sherlock Homes (mom), sports (dad), books on business and fun romps in literature. We have an original, first printing of the Complete Works of James Fenimore Cooper, now in my possession, which has been in the family for more than a hundred years. Books are our treasure. My reading habits might more reflect the folks as I have the time, due to travel and the percentage of the day devoted to the actual job, but I remember fondly trips to the library and summer reading programs when I was a kid.

As the years became heavier they only read more. It was almost as if mom knew time was running faster than she could anymore and she wanted to devour as many books as she could fit on the plate. To this day if you go to Dad's house you will find a fresh stack of books on the coffee table and scattered about the house. They loved to read, there, I said it again. And laugh!

It was a house filled with laughter. Not twenty-four hours every day, that would be an asylum, but they loved comedy. They had records by the masters; Bob Newhart, Shelly Berman, Bill Cosby, yeah, that Bill Cosby, when he was funny not creepy, The Goon Shows, with Spike Milligan and Peter Sellers, the 'Blue' records of Redd Foxx, hysterical songs by Tom Lehrer, Spike Jones, Allen Sherman and Jackie Vernon, Jonathon and Darlene Edwards, Stan Freberg and Nichols and May. I would sit on the stairs where they couldn't see me and listen as they laughed hysterically through an evening with friends, cocktails and comedy.

They loved the movies of Abbot and Costello or the more cerebral comedy of Laurel and Hardy, The Pink Panther series with Peter Sellers, Airplane and Blazing Saddles. Mom would quote these movies and comedy records when making points and then just laugh. And, of course, The Marx Brothers, the best and funniest of them all. I though the folks, and especially mom, was going to bust a gut every time one of the flicks would come on the tube. As much as mom enjoyed the Cerebral she loved her slapstick. Spoken word or visual, well played scene or silence meant to evoke joy, it would depend on mood and circumstance, but all just made them roar.

And then, it was gone.

The Newest Chapter, Late

Dad was now 83 years old and on his own for the first time since June 7, 1947 and at a bit of a loss as to what to do with himself. He had his friends and neighbors, that was a given, they would stand by him, so he would not want for company. But he didn't want to just survive, to live out his days.

I received a phone call one afternoon as I was puttering about the house. It was an oddity that I was home as, like my father, I spent most of my time on the road.

"You're going to think I'm nuts," began the conversation.

"Dad, in math we say, 'that's a given,'" I reply, "you've been nuts since I've known you."

"Well, you know I always promised your mother that I would go back to college and get my degree?" he paused.

"Yes," I encouraged, now knowing where this was headed.

"I've decided to go to college and get the degree." He let it drop.

"Excellent!"

"Well, it's been a while since she's been gone, and I've given it a lot of thought," he continued, justifying his decision to me but really to himself, "they'll let me audit the classes for free but then I don't get credit, I don't get to graduate and receive a diploma." He stopped again.

"So."

"So, I've decided I am going to pay for it, so I can get the piece of paper." He waited.

"I think that's fantastic!" As I did, "What's everybody else saying?"

"They want to know when graduation is, so they can make plans," he grinned through the phone and barked a laugh. "so, I'm spending your inheritance on school!"

"We all think you should do what you want and spend your money as you see fit. It's your money not ours, we didn't earn it." Which truly is the sentiment in our family, want to leave a legacy, bequeath us photos and stories of places we should go and things we should see.

This was a wonderful idea in many ways, shapes and forms. Number one, dad was finally opening up more and more to us about who he was. I have mentioned several times that neither of the folks were big on public displays nor sharing feelings. I believe it was a generational thing as well as how both were brought up. Dad in a restrained Dutch home and mom in a German/Irish atmosphere, one side shut off from overwrought feeling the other drinking, singing and wanting to hug you. But both of the parental units were private individuals. If you earned praise or attention it was fine, within bounds, but other than that, nothing to see here.

My brother David had a small surprise birthday for mom one year, nothing grandiose, he didn't rent a hall and a band, just some folks over to his house to celebrate mom's birth. She was not happy about it though didn't show it at the party. But just felt he shouldn't have gone to all the trouble just for her. Very typical of how she felt about things. We were shocked when she allowed us all to celebrate her 80th birthday, just family, no friends, but we were all there. Children, Grandchildren, it was a passel of people. We believe she agreed because it was being held upstairs at Johnny's on Fulton, her favorite restaurant in the world. Dad dropped some coinage that day!

But again, she was not showy, didn't want a lot of fuss. Somehow dad convinced her, and, apparently, he spent a good portion of his life trying to convince her to do something he thought might be fun, to allow him to have parties to celebrate their 50th and 60th wedding anniversaries. She didn't see the need. They could just go out to dinner and be done with it. I believe he called down intervention from Heaven and, also, promised there would be no buffet. Mom didn't care for buffets, these would be sit down dinner affairs. All had a marvelous time, including mom, and all agreed it was necessary. Staying together for 50 years deserved notice. Staying married to my father for 60 deserved Sainthood.

So, off to college went the nervous freshman. I don't think I have ever witnessed my father nervous about anything in his life, but he actually was nervous about this. He hadn't been in a classroom, except to pick up mom from work, for more than fifty years. He was pretty sure things had changed. And, he was all but computer illiterate.

He struggled. He struggled with the curriculum, he struggled with the technology, he struggled with the youth and vigor of those who raced by him on campus. He began to doubt the wisdom of his course of action. Did he consider quitting? One would think so, but one wouldn't know my father. He may have mentioned the stress and strain of trying to keep up with these kids. He may have even mentioned how he felt as if he didn't belong here. He may have voiced questions of his sanity, out loud and in public, once or twice for attempting this at his age, but he would never quit. It just isn't in the man.

He stayed after classes and asked his professors for help. He did not, would not, ask them to ease up, just help him get in the right mindset. He asked them to teach him what he might be missing. To explain what was whizzing by his head in the classroom. To catch him up on fifty years of new knowledge and new techniques he hadn't considered for a half century. Gladly they obliged. Not because of his age or who he might have been or done but because they saw he wanted it. He wanted to learn like a young sapling needs water. He wouldn't quit, he would find a way, and they were ecstatic to provide the tools and path, so he could succeed. And the other students, the young, vigorous, vibrant, just coming out of twelve years of the same curriculum, maybe taking their education for granted, the kids, saw what he was willing to do to learn and they couldn't help but follow this ancient man.

They jumped in to help him with technology that hadn't even been a dream when he had last attended college. They were patient and caring and wanted him to succeed as much as their professors. And he taught them as well. Not college things, not numbers and letters and such but life. He showed them what a life well lived could be. He personified hard work, perseverance, a willingness to go against the odds and take a chance. Risk is not a bad thing, it excites and gets the adrenaline racing. If you are not willing to challenge yourself how will you stand up when the world, life, others, challenge you?

He taught them their history and by doing so taught them their hopes and dreams for their future could be realized. This 85-year-old man was the essence of vitality and spirit and would win out in the end; or die trying.

So, they hung around him. We were talking one day, and he laughed as he explained that he didn't know if the kids really liked him or they just hung around because he was good for lunch. They seemed to materialize as he would head to the cafeteria and line up behind him, looking hungry and broke. He laughed harder as he told me how he couldn't let his kids go hungry. He knew he was being conned and scammed, and they knew he knew, and it just didn't matter. It was cheap, and they were helping him learn; and he was helping them become better people. They all ate lunch together, talking and laughing as normal college students do. When was the last time you got to sit and share a meal and conversation with your favorite grandpa?

He solidified his relationship with the students who shared lecture halls with him, as well as his history professor, one day as the professor was discussing a battle during WWII. She explained how the battle went, what it was like, why it was happening, all kinds of good information. My dad raised his hand warily.

"Yes, Bob, what is it?" she asked.

"That's not how it happened," he stated

"Not how what happened?" she kind of smirked sensing where this might be going.

"Well, not how that battle happened," he replied.

"Yes, it is, there have been many studies about this particular battle," she smiled.

"Well, I'm here to tell that is not how things were," he insisted.

"And, how would you know that," she prodded.

"I was there. I fought in that battle and how you're describing it was not how things went."

The questions began immediately. We think sometimes students are slackers or not paying attention. Well, they instantly realized they had the greatest resource they could ever find sitting right next to them, and they were going to make use of it. Mr. Popular became much more popular. Truly BMOC.

I believe it was how my father presented his case rather than what was said. He has always been a believer in the fact you cannot teach someone whom you just irritated or pissed off. If he had been more aggressive in his correction of the professor, it would only have led to an argument and a heated back and forth. By explaining and sharing everyone benefitted and the professor gave way to the true expert on the subject. Both looked like stars.

Dad liked to show people what he meant rather than shove it down their throats. When he was a mighty muck-a-muck with the trucking company he wanted to get across the concept of customer service to his employees and how important it was. So, he would ask a new hire, or someone they might be having a problem getting to understand this concept, to wait for him in a conference room. He would explain that he had one more interview to finish up, or he had to make an important phone call, before he got to said meeting, but he would be in momentarily. Just one thing, though, if the phone rang, please answer it and take a message as he was waiting for another important call.

The applicant would go into the room and make themselves comfortable and wait. Within a few minutes, sure enough, the phone would ring. They would answer it, pen and paper at the ready, to show they could follow instructions. The person on the other end would ask for Mr. Zonneville. The 'student' would reply he wasn't here, could he take a message. And the caller would say yes, take this down. He would begin to dictate and then be interrupted by someone on his end. 'Is it OK if I put you on hold for a minute?' he would ask. 'Of course.'

Now understand, there were no clocks in the conference room and the applicant was not allowed to have a watch on either. So, he would sit at the ready while holding. After a while my dad would walk in and tell them to hang up. 'How long were you on hold?' dad asked. The responses would vary anywhere from ten to twenty minutes. 'You were on hold for three minutes,' dad would say. 'That's impossible,' they would sputter, 'it felt like forever.' 'Yes, it does, when you leave someone on hold for any length of time. When you are talking to a customer never put them on hold, never leave them hanging as it says two things to them. Number one, they are not your top priority and number two, you think you can do better elsewhere.' He smiled. 'At Spector/INWAY/wherever the customer is always your first priority. If someone calls while you are on the line with a customer, ask whoever took the call to take a number and you'll get right back to them.' Lesson over. And for those of you that have been left on hold for any length of time you know this would be a better world if everyone would take this to heart.

Once he got into the rhythm of college and began to understand and use the technology, though he will never be a techno wiz, he began to really enjoy the experience. He loved the young folks he associated with every day. They returned the feeling. They continued to be as patient in their instructions as he had been with his stories. It was truly a symbiotic relationship, each contributing to the advancement of the other. My father would gush on how smart these kids were, how sharp they were, they picked things right up. We would explain they had been in classes just last year, and for the twelve years leading up to that year, it had not been since before their parents were born. Learning, like anything else in life, is so much easier when you are used to the routine.

He loved the students and treasured his time around them. "I'm a great believer in the younger generation." He pontificated one day. "I wish I was as smart as they are. I have a ball with them. They're very bright and I'm glad I'm not in competition with them. Too often we criticize them, failing to realize how bright and good they are. Seriously, I think we overlook them; these kids are fantastic. I am very confident with our future in their hands."

Dad graduated with an associate of arts degree on May 11, 2013 from Lakeland Community College. At the time he was the oldest graduate in the history of Ohio. Only to be beat out soon after by Morton Mandel, who happens to be the father of dear friend of mine, Thom Mandel. Couldn't even give us a full week to celebrate!

My father considers this to be one of his greatest accomplishments, not only because he can point to the piece of paper that claims him a college graduate, but what he had to go through to earn it. It was a lifetime in the making, three years of testing himself and his resolve in his late eighties', getting to meet, yeah, that again, and know all these professors, administrators and students. And, I believe, mostly, because he fulfilled a promise, a vow, to his late wife. It was truly a day of celebration, joy and pride for dad, his children, grandchildren and great grandchildren, most of whom made it to the graduation ceremony.

During his college career of dad was like any other student in many ways. He studied, he worked hard, he held down a couple of jobs (volunteer), went out for the occasional beer and met a sweetheart. You read it right, he met a sweetheart at 88 years old. Why not?

Dad had now lived alone for five years. He appeared content, but I don't think anyone really believed the act. You cannot share your life, your hopes, your inner most thoughts, fears, triumphs, failures and successes, with another human being then have that person suddenly pulled from your day to day and not have it affect you. You turn to say something to someone who isn't sitting where they should be. You hear a noise in the other room or upstairs and think, are they home? Every place you look, every time you sit to read or watch a game, they're not there. Loneliness takes on many façades, the most common is one of 'I'm fine'.

He did well to immerse himself in the life-giving waters of study, classrooms and the young. He buried his needs in volunteering at

Hospice, the VFW, American Legion and giving of himself to others. It was easy, it was what he'd done his whole life. He loved helping those less fortunate, those who needed the hand, the ear, the support he could give. Why not just continue? But it really is never enough to fool ourselves completely.

About this time a young fella had moved in diagonally across the street from pops and, as usual, my father had gotten to know him. Dad would be out walking the dog, or just hanging around the neighborhood helping someone with some chore, and he'd run into this young man, they would share a word or two, or three or a conversation. It's in his DNA! Vytas Saldukas had emigrated from Lithuania. He was a hard-working, talented, craftsman. He did carpentry, finishing, dry wall, floors, painting, you name it, though he mostly did roofs. Dad and Vytas had become, not close, but friendly, as he was with all his neighbors. Vytas was a sociable person who enjoyed helping out his neighbors when he could. The kind of person my father always gravitated towards.

One day dad was out walking the dog through the neighborhood and he saw a woman weeding the gardens around Vytas' home. She was not your typical landscape looking worker. A little older than most people who do this kind of work; though Betsy worked in a nursery, so, maybe.

A few days later he was walking through the neighborhood and stopped to talk to Bob Krizancic, Coach K from the Mentor basketball program, and also a neighbor, and he noticed this woman again as he walked back towards home. She smiled, friendly, and looked at dad and motioned toward the house while saying, 'tea?' It was quite obvious she spoke very little English but was trying. Dad shook his head no and made a face to express his distaste for the stuff. 'Coffee?' she asked. Of course. We never turn down coffee. She seemed like such a nice person trying to make contact with someone, anyone, who were neighbors. He was to learn through a word here, a gesture there, that she was Vytas' mother visiting from Lithuania.

Dad ran into Vytas a few days later and Vytas explained that his mother was a teacher in Lithuania and was just visiting for the summer before heading home for another year before retiring from education. He was trying to find her a part time job, so she could make a few dollars of her own while here. Besides, as active as she always was, she would be bored silly if she just sat around the house while Vytas was at work. His mother was a person who did not take to leisure and inactivity. She was a very independent woman and didn't want to rely on him for her needs, she wished to make her own money. And she enjoyed working.

Dad suggested, if she wouldn't mind, he needed someone to help take care his house. He has this large, four-bedroom place and it was getting to be a bit much for him. Even he had to admit he couldn't do at 88 what he had done at 78. He would gladly pay her, and she would be right across the street from where she was living. She wouldn't need a ride, she would be in her comfort zone, close to home if she needed anything, and wouldn't feel bad about her limited English. A win-win for all involved. Vytas took the idea to his mom, she loved it and the deal was set for her to come over a couple times a week and help him out.

I need to mention that at his time all intent was as innocent and businesslike as can be. These were just two people who could benefit from a working relationship and they would become friends along the way. She could practice her English while over at his place and not feel embarrassed or out of place. Though learning English from my father might not be the best idea! She would be swearing like a sailor within the month!

At one-point dad asked Elvyra, if she would like to grab a salad for lunch. It took a little dancing and gesturing and broken English, but he got the point across. It would just be a little lunch, he wasn't trying to 'put the moves' on her, just a kind of 'thank you' for all she had been doing. Every time she came over she brought fresh cooked Lithuanian fare and pastries. She would always make sure he was eating, and they would visit and just share each other's company. She agreed, and they took off for Ruby Tuesday's.

Vytas confronted him about this the next day. "You took my mother to lunch?" he asked.

Wow, had dad overstepped the bounds of neighbor and part time employer. He liked Vytas, he didn't want him to think he was trying to take advantage of his mom! He didn't really know anything about her, she just seemed as if she could use a friend. He didn't mean anything by it.

"Yes," he confessed.

"Good," Vytas replies, "my father passed away many years ago and she would never even talk to another man. I have been trying to get her to just go out with friends, to socialize, to meet people. I think she has been lonely since he passed but would not go out, or anything, as she was raising us by herself. I don't think she believed it was proper. Her first and most important responsibility was to us. We were very small when he died, she raised the three of us alone. We all wished she would do something for herself, to enjoy her life a little. Not just worry about her children"

What could dad say? He was even more impressed with this woman than he'd originally thought. She returned to Lithuania, and home, soon after. She would teach for another year and then retire and come back to Mentor to stay with Vytas for a while.

But Vytas was young, good looking, hard-working and, well, young. He loved his mother, we all do, but he would like her to maybe not be living with him at this time of life. Dad to the rescue. He explains to Vytas he has this huge house all to himself. If Elvyra would like she can have her own room, shit, she could have her own set of rooms, her own bathroom, all she would need, particularly her privacy. If it would help Vytas. And if she would like to stay there. She can earn her room and board by doing what she had before, helping him to clean and take care of the home. Vytas likes the idea but would his mom?

So, my father emailed her in Lithuania with this brilliant plan. She emails back her uncertainty. He emails that Vytas thinks it's a good idea. She emails her uncertainty. You get the idea. Finally, she emails him with this idea, she has been to America and knows what it is like, why doesn't he come to Lithuania and meet her family, so he can see what her home is like? He can meet her family, and they him, they can all get each other's measure, and decide, together, if they think this is as brilliant as young Vytas and Old Bob. So, sure, why not? He wasn't really doing anything anyway. He finds a hole in his schedule where there is no school and the world can do without his volunteering for a few days and agrees to come visit.

I don't know if I have mentioned, but my father can be a bit impetuous. Off to Lithuania to meet family and friends. They wine and dine him on the finest of home cooked Lithuanian foods. He tours a good portion of the country. Finds out how much he he loves it. Lithuania is a beautiful place with wonderful, warm, gregarious people. He assumes they are not saying horrible things about him, though he can't be absolutely certain, as they speak no English and his Lithuanian is non-existent. But there is copious laughter and a general feeling of good will, so he assumes all is well.

They return from Lithuania and she moves in. A plutonic relationship of two folks just looking for a little companionship on the journey. Friends sharing a drink and some life. They share their meals and their time. Dad drives her around if she needs to do errands, she cooks, cleans, reads and they become a bit more comfortable with each other's presence.

Well, they became friends, good friends, he was helping her with her English, they bought a Rosetta Stone program for her, and she kept him in line. Elvyra is a very strong willed, humorous, fun woman. She loves to laugh but she won't put up with any shit from anybody, especially my father. They made a good team. We all thought so. We like her a lot. We think she is a special person. And, apparently so did dad.

As he was getting ready to graduate they were sitting after dinner having cocktails and he asked her if she ever thought about getting married again. She explained she had been alone a very long time and, no, she really hadn't given it much thought. She, naturally, assumed he hadn't either, as he was up in years and mom had only passed five or so years ago. Why would he ask? He told her why. I guess the best term that would describe her reaction was shocked. But upon further consideration, she said yes. They called a friend of his, Judge Tremitz, to perform the intimate ceremony. Her choice.

People would ask all the time why dad would remarry at his age. To which I reply because that is what people do when they graduate from college, they get married! And I do mean right after they graduate. They were married three weeks after he graduated.

Was I bothered my father would get married again? Not in the least and neither were any of my brothers or sister, we all wanted one thing, for dad to be happy. And this woman made him happy, kept him in line and would now add years to his life. For that we can only be thankful. Plus, we really like her! I should mention they did call her children, Vytas and Berta, his new beautiful wife, and living across the street, beginning their own family. Soon to include Augustas and Carolina. The engaged couple then called her son Marius and his wife, Kotrina, who live in Northern Ireland and, finally, Elvyra's daughter Mireta, in Lithuania. Amazingly all were delighted with the turn of events. It would seem all on both sides of the Atlantic, were quite enthused about the joining of families.

If anyone was upset, it was the grand kids. How could grandpa get married again? How could he forget grandma? He would never forget Carol, grandma to the grand kids and mom to us, she was the love of his life, but she was not coming back, I explained. Did they want him to be miserable? Sad? Moping around that big old house by himself? No? Then they should be ecstatic that he had found someone willing to put up with him and who made him happy. They would get to keep their grandfather around for far longer because Elvyra was in his life. End of story.

Z

Oh, Wait a Minute!

But this story is not over. He is still spry and energetic, on the ball at 93 years old. He is still a pain in the butt, loud, opinionated, smart, generous, giving of his time and knowledge. He still talks about the future. He doesn't forget the past he just chooses not to live there.

Oh, he remembers. He remembers with all the passion any human being can summon for all he has done in his life. He remembers being hungry and cold as a child. Working for a couple hours before going to a one room schoolhouse and then returning home to chores.

He'd been almost killed delivering papers as a boy. Had lived to fight in the war and get wounded twice. He'd succeeded and failed many times in life. What is life without some failure? Where would you learn about yourself? How do you test your true mettle without adversity?

And he'd known love; twice. He was, as he loves to say over and over, the luckiest man alive. He'd been married to my mother for 61 years and has now been married to Elvyra for 5. Life is nothing if not fluid. Death comes too quick to stop living now.

They spent New Year's in Northern Ireland with her son, Marius. And got to return, for the first time, to where he'd been stationed before the Normandy landing. They seem to enjoy each other's company and they live. They go out, once in a while, to dinner though Elvyra is a stickler for home cooking. She sees no reason to go out somewhere when you can enjoy a relaxed evening with family at home. Especially when she can cook up a banquet that no restaurant can touch. It is loud, there is laughter and children under foot, the food keeps coming and it is family.

Now, it is a family that stretches not only across this country but Ireland, Poland and Lithuania. The Lakota of the plains natives have a saying, 'Mitakuye Oyasin.' It simply means 'we are all related' and our family continues to prove that true.

I have discovered Zonneville's that we are related to in France. Where, actually, the family began before being chased out by the French in 1680. We were Huguenots, who knew? The French representative who pinned the Legion of Honor on my father did, that's who! There are relatives in Oklahoma, Jacqueline, third cousins or something but we are all from the same great grandfather. And there is my Texas family, with one child over in Florida, Dana Brown, where she resides with her husband, Dustin, and two children, Keegan and Logan. The rest, I finally got to meet a few years ago down in Houston and have been back several times since. There is Deborah, wife to Robert Black, a fantastic guy, and mother to Jonathon and older sister Jerica. She is now married to Steven Stroud, also from upstate New York, and his son Owen, he is a delightful child I have had the pleasure of hanging with a couple times! We drink wine and bourbon, eat and get loud and argue. We are Zonneville's.

My father could not write this book. That is a fact. It is almost impossible to write about yourself. My father is not a humble man, he knows where he came from and what he has accomplished but he is not a braggart. Facts are facts and what you have read here are just the facts of his life, no brag just the truth. All colored by the love of a son and his, sometimes, flawed memories.

He is not a Saint, but he has given back to his country, his family, his community, in thanks, for all he, and his family, was given and have received. He earned what he has, make no mistake about that. He worked his ass off, nights, days and in between. He picked up whatever kind of job that would put food on the table.

He weeded farms, not gardens, farms. He was a migrant worker picking cherries, apples, strawberries, tomatoes and peaches. Recently my uncle Richard passed away and at the funeral parlor my dad introduced me to a man whose family he had picked cherries for 80 years before. This fella couldn't say enough about the Zonneville clan's work ethic, though some needed a swift kick in the pants from time to time, as well as my mother's. He spoke of my mom and dad out in the hot sun, side by side, doing these back breaking chores, never complaining just giving a full day's work for a full day's pay. And remember my mother came from money, and here she was out in the hot orchard filling bushel baskets with cherries and apples. It is hard thankless work, but it helps pay the bills. This man still remembered my dad because he was a hard worker who gave his full measure. That is something to be remembered for.

He has now outlived most of his old friends. And I mean outlived. He rode in a hot balloon over France, in 2002. His granddaughter Adrienne bought him a ride in a stock car, NASCAR style, where they ran around Charlotte Motor Speedway several times at racing speed.

A man he knew, who had way more money than my father could imagine, a multi-millionaire, used to say to him, "Bob, you live life like no one I know." Meanwhile, the gentleman spoken of never did anything fun. Wouldn't go out to a nice dinner for fear of spending the money. Never traveled, just stayed home. He would contribute to whatever cause my pops was collecting for, but just enough. One day dad took him out for a nice dinner, on him, of course, just so the guy could experience for himself the difference between enjoying life and just going through it. The fellow couldn't believe it. Went on for days about how wonderful this meal had been. I don't think he ever changed his ways, but my father tried. As has been mentioned here, my father never had a ton of cash, but he never let that get in the way of life.

"What's the use of having all that money," he would say, shaking his head, "if you don't enjoy it?"

He believed as deeply as if it was part of his DNA, you could never do enough to help others. In 1990 he and Bob Murphy put together a Golf outing in the memory of Jackie McKinley, she had been quite active in Hospice for years. She and her husband had been regulars on the travels with Bob and Bob tours. These two knuckleheads kept the outing going until 2004 when Murphy passed away. Dad kept it up for a few more years but it just kind of dwindled. Though over the years they raised over a quarter-million-dollars for Hospice of Western Reserve.

He was elected into the Lake County Council on Aging's Hall of Fame. His positive attitude, his unwillingness to quit, were his greatest qualifications. He walks several miles a day, either outside when weather permits or on his treadmill. He never stops, he is always engaged either in raising funds for Mentor and Lake Catholic government clubs, The Honor Flights, not as a recipient but as a chaperone. Oh, and he pays his own way, that's how it works. He gives his time and energy to Hospice of the Western Reserve as a volunteer specializing in comforting and spending time with veterans; World War II Vets, Korean War, Vietnam, all the wars, all his comrades in arms. They so appreciate having someone who knows, truly knows, what they lived, to talk with, share time with, as they near the end of the trail. It is his specialty, caring. He received four Peaceful and Proud Designations. It is a national award dedicated to those who Provide for Veterans end of life care. He sits vigils with these Veterans, so they know someone is with them when the end comes, and then sits and consoles the families. He provides information the Vets and their families might not be aware of and wouldn't receive without his intervention.

He always has a smile and a hello for anyone in his path; butcher, baker, checkout clerk, business owner, mayor, president, street sweeper, he doesn't discriminate. Oh, he sometimes has other words for those who displease him or get in his way but just on occasion. But, hey, he was also voted one of the most interesting people in Northeast Ohio by Cleveland magazine in 1978. Not the nicest, not the most boring, one of the most interesting!

Here's one for ya, he plays Santa at both the Mentor Civic Center and Euclid daycares as well as for the neighborhood for 25 years, and even played the Easter Bunny once or twice. I know, I know I can't quite imagine it either. He spends his own money to purchase

Christmas gifts and candy for the less fortunate and with the help of Boulevard Presbyterian Church provides a Christmas for those in poverty, sometimes providing the only gifts any of these folks will see. He considers it just a way of spending his children's inheritance! Spend away, Bob, and enjoy.

He has been involved in Boulevard Presbyterian since we first moved to Euclid in '62 and, are you ready for this, has preached services several times. And the building still stands!

Trust me he still enjoys a cocktail or two with friends or when he and Elvyra finish dinner. He does not suffer fools gladly. He has always expected everyone to give their best effort in any endeavor. Whether running a company, washing dishes, or anything in between. You may not be good at something, you may never get good at that assignment, but he expected you to give your full and best stab at the task. He could never fault you if you gave an honest effort. Maybe that is where I arrived at my philosophy that everyone has genius for something. You just have to find it; find your passion and you will find your genius. If you try your best you might find you really enjoy a vocation you never considered before. I have known people who were brilliant songwriters, artists, mechanics and janitors. They all loved what they did, and they gave it their all, every day, and did it well. And if you have job you don't like, it still doesn't give you carte blanche to half-ass it. The folks who hire you deserve your best, if you can't do that leave and let someone else do the job.

He is not perfect. I have written that several times in this tome and I cannot say it enough. He is finest man I have ever known, he is who I look up to most, with my big brother second. He is generous to a fault and has never been cruel. But his expectations are high, especially for himself, and so will cut you very little slack. If he has to live up to his standards why shouldn't you. He is very tough but always fair. He was with his children, his employees, his friends and those he associates with on a day to day basis.

You can no longer do any of this; but, I remember one time being with him in a grocery store and a child was acting up. He was maybe four or five and just stomping and screaming and running around the store. His mother seemed not to notice. Everyone else within a quarter mile did, but this mom would give the kid some candy to settle him down for a minute and just went about her business. Finally, dad had enough. I thought he was going to go over and whack either the kid or the mom. But he didn't! He walked over, cornered the kid and firmly, but wrapped in a thin coating of gentle, explained to the young man this was not how we behave in public. The mother finally comes over to chastise dad for talking to her kid and his look stopped her. Again, with kindness he explained that he understood it is hard and exhausting to raise children, and here he points at me, but she is not doing the child any favors by allowing him to throw a tantrum and run roughshod through life. Whether she wished to or not she simply had to instill some discipline or there would be hell to pay later in life for her and the kid. She isn't doing herself or the rest of society any favors either. By now the kid had settled down, without reward, and the woman thanked dad for caring. She was just so tired. He understood, he truly did, but that is the price of children, he laughed, and pointed in my direction again. Sometimes it takes a village, sometimes it just takes someone who cares.

That is my father, yesterday and today. Whether he was president of the company, dock worker, harvesting next to his father, making the run to NY or Philly, fighting a war or keeping the peace between union and management, he listened considered and did his best to be evenhanded.

As a father he was absent physically, due to the job, but he was always with us. He called home and when he was home he was engaged. He showed up at ballgames and whatever else were involved in. He couldn't always be there, but we knew he was in spirit.

We've had our scares, sorrow and missteps. We almost lost David in 2016 due to an accident at work. And even over the months it took for him to recover we couldn't be sure he would be himself if he did. It was a massive head injury. We visited almost every day, if one couldn't be at his bedside someone else would make certain they showed up. It was scary for all concerned. Happy to report he is doing well and feeling fine. Granddaughter Ellen had a wee bout with the cancer bug in 2018 but, now, seems to be chugging along just swell.

Bets and Bob now have seven Grandchildren. Ellen and her husband at the time, John Geiger, gave them Jack in 2003, CJ in 2007 and Isabella in 2009. Her new husband, whom she married in January of 2017, Master Sargent Matt Kohn brought along his lovely daughter, Madison. Greg and Jess Schulz have added Jackson born in 2011, Sam in 2014 and the beautiful Madeleine in 2017 to the grandchildren pool. Me thinks they need a bigger pool! Robin and Manette have one but he's more than a match for all of them. AJ is the light of their, and Jennifer's, lives, he entered this unprepared world on 2013, you may have felt the quake.

As mentioned earlier we lost uncle Richard in March of 2018. Funerals are hard, sad, horrible affairs but you get to reconnect with the living. Odd isn't it? It takes death for us to remember how much we love those still alive and how much they mean to us. Mayhap we should take time well before the funeral to reconnect. But it was wonderful to see and talk with Aunt Martha, though the circumstances do not lend themselves to a long enjoyable visit. I got to meet Sandy's and Susan's daughters, they are lovely, intelligent well-spoken young women and make the family proud. Spent time with cousin Penny and visited with cousin Charlie with his wife Donna. Reminiscing and sharing stories and updates on all our kids. If not for the fact a favorite uncle had died it would have been a wonderful visit. Such is life.

How is a life defined? Is the definition of a life well lived great accomplishments? Those few moments you believe will live forever? The touchdown catch that wins the game? A home run in the bottom of the ninth? Winning a race? Do you have to be Lincoln, FDR or Boone for your life to matter? A star of stage, screen or TV to be defined a success? To some, yes, they feel that is the only symbol. Wealth and fame. And yet, all of those people have problems, faults, failures, and breakdowns and don't appear any happier than most of us.

My father's life is not defined by great moments in time, though he participated in some of the most significant in history. His life has been defined by a thousand moments. By countless acts of kindness and friendship. By the day to day work ethic that was ingrained in him by his father. He was respected by his friends and co-workers, high and low, and that is something to hang your hat on. Fame is fleeting, respect is forever.

He gave of himself by volunteering and lifting others up. He fought in the great war but was just a cog in the machine. Though we all know cogs run the machine. He was decent, worked hard, raised his family, treated people fair and well. He walked the walk each and every day, week and month of his life. He inspired others. Did he change history? Did greatness eddy around him? Did time stop? Nope. But he did change the futures of those he came in contact with. Some just an inch, some by one hundred and eighty degrees. He never asked for anything in return and never complained when life dealt him a bad hand. Like his father before him, he shut up, put his shoulder to the wheel and pushed a little harder.

And he got his just rewards. He was successful in his life. He accomplished his goals and he brought, mostly, joy into others lives. He got invited to the groundbreaking ceremony for the World War II memorial and dedication in Washington, D.C. Picked up and hauled around by a General Edmundson and Colonel Larson, not bad for an old Staff Sergeant and hole digger in the war. And spoke to members of the Canadian Parliament about affairs related to the trucking industry in North America. Somebody wanted to listen to a man who knew of what he spoke.

Are there more important things in life? I can't say, I wouldn't know what they might be.

He has never, to my knowledge, been jealous of another's success and never begrudged anyone their just rewards for hard work and perseverance. If they earned it, he was overjoyed to celebrate another's accomplishments. Will he be sung about in songs and stories told? Actually, yes. I have written two songs about my father, 'Bear Swamp Road' and 'Ordinary People'. So there! And here is a book celebrating his life. Not bad for a poor, dumb, old farm boy, son of immigrant parents and poverty, from upstate New York, who was born, literally, without a pot to piss in.

And he and mom must have done something right in life, must

have set a fine example of how to live, as their children and grandchildren have found happiness in life. Sister Betsy still works at the nursery thanks to a few new parts and an overhaul of her hips. I believe she, like her father, will continue to work until someone loads her on a wheelbarrow and hauls her away. Her husband Bob is kind of semi-retired, doing consulting work and very involved in robotics competitions with his, very young proteges! They recently traveled to Austria, Germany and Prague.

Their daughter Ellen is happily married to Matt and the mother of four wonderful children. She is a senior Business Systems Analyst for Epic Healthcare Platform. She has spent the last fourteen years crisscrossing the country working at Tucson Medical Center, Dean Hospital, Banner, The Cleveland Clinic, University of Colorado, Lancaster General and The UCSD. Apparently, the gypsy gene is strong in this one as she also enjoys traveling to all four corners of the world. Husband Matt has served his country for 18 years. Four years active duty and the last fourteen with the reserves and Guard. He is a Master Sergeant and work group leader.

Her brother Greg assembled bone density scanners and refurbished ultrasound units for GE Healthcare from 2005 through 2012. He moved into tech support and field service on those same bone density scanners and from there he jumped to sales. He now is a regional Account Manager for Diesel Forward and is a price strategist. He, like all in this family, loves to travel and has been to Europe several times enjoying the beers of the German homeland. The lovely Jessica also put in her time with Diesel Forward from 2005 through 2017 but has three fantastic kids who require her full attention at home. I am assuming she misses the quiet of the job!

Robin and Manette are now both retired from very satisfying careers. He in automotive repair business, which he would've continued forever had not the years of standing and working on concrete floors and fighting engines, transmissions and suspension systems, bending in every imaginable contortion, taken such a harsh toll on his body. Manette worked for years for Rockwell International in the HR department before deciding they should spend some time traveling and being grandma and grandpa to AJ, son of Jennifer. She of the green bean fame, she is a wiz when it come to the cultivation, harvesting and distribution of the best green beans in the world. It's kind of a specialty because she just loves it. She and John Torrese also own and manage the Oswego Raceway. He and his brother own acres of farmland in Florida. In her spare time, Jennifer works for the city of Oswego New York. She apparently is easily bored.

David is back to work at Sidley's where he runs a material yard focusing on limestone, blocks and crushed, tools and supplies for road construction. After wandering, as so many of us do, in the wasteland of employment, programming, tech support and repair in the computer industry, gas jockey, he discovered he had a knack for the building material trade and is quite happy. He and Cindy enjoy a life on the far eastside of Cleveland.

I am still on the road entertaining the masses and my wife continues to work in the hospitality industry. We both love to travel and live as if we had money. It's a family tradition! Daughter Adrienne worked as a mechanic for NASCAR teams for 12 years and has now been with Sieman's building turbines running a machine that is larger than my house. She has a house washing business on the side and travels every chance she gets. Sister Kate worked for the corporate world until she'd had her fill. She quit and bought her own Lularoe franchise and now gets to work in her pajamas, set her own hours and worry about being self-employed. Husband Jim is retired from the trucking industry and golfing. They both are loving life!

So, the clan continues, and we are happy, the bills are mostly paid, travels and adventure continue, and our children grow fat and filled with joy.

I would have to say my parents were in the Hall of Fame for parenting!

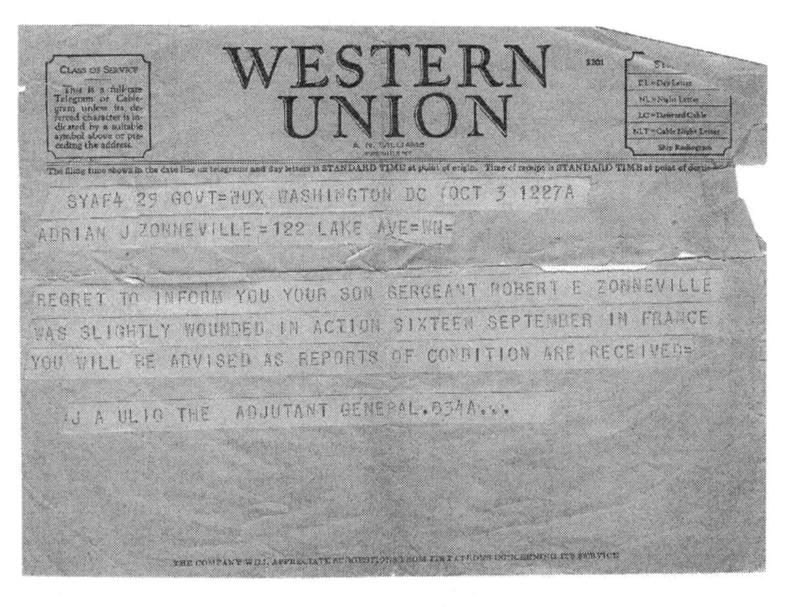

WESTERN UNION

CLASS OF SERVICE

This is a full-rate Telegram or Cablegram unless its deferred character is indicated by a suitable symbol above or preceding the address.

DL = Day Letter
NL = Night Letter
LC = Deferred Cable
NLT = Cable Night Letter
Ship Radiogram

The filing time shown in the date line on telegrams and day letters is STANDARD TIME at point of origin. Time of receipt is STANDARD TIME at point of destination

SYAF4 29 GOVT=WUX WASHINGTON DC OCT 3 1227A

ADRIAN J ZONNEVILLE =122 LAKE AVE=WN=

REGRET TO INFORM YOU YOUR SON SERGEANT ROBERT E ZONNEVILLE
WAS SLIGHTLY WOUNDED IN ACTION SIXTEEN SEPTEMBER IN FRANCE
YOU WILL BE ADVISED AS REPORTS OF CONDITION ARE RECEIVED=

J A ULIO THE ADJUTANT GENERAL.

RF

RÉPUBLIQUE FRANÇAISE

ORDRE NATIONAL DE LA LÉGION D'HONNEUR

HONNEUR PATRIE

LE PRÉSIDENT DE LA RÉPUBLIQUE FRANÇAISE

GRAND MAÎTRE DE L'ORDRE NATIONAL DE LA LÉGION D'HONNEUR

nomme, par décret de ce jour, Monsieur Robert E. ZONNEVILLE

Vétéran de la deuxième guerre mondiale
de nationalité américaine

CHEVALIER DE LA LÉGION D'HONNEUR

Fait à PARIS, le 20 août 2013

Scellé du sceau de l'Ordre sous le n° 1095SLHE13
p/le Secrétaire Général Adjoint,

Laurent BLONDEAU-GEORGES

Par le Président de la République :
LE GRAND CHANCELIER DE LA LÉGION D'HONNEUR,

Général d'armée GEORGELIN

OHIO SENATE

HONORING
ROBERT ZONNEVILLE
FOR EXEMPLARY SERVICE

On behalf of the members of the Senate of the 132nd General Assembly of Ohio, we are pleased to extend special recognition to Robert Zonneville on being named a Hero for Andy by the Andy Nowacki Foundation, Inc., April 8, 2017.

Your selfless contributions to the Hospice of the Western Reserve have been integral to upholding the establishment's mission to celebrate the individual worth of each life, and you have purposefully drawn from your wealth of intrinsic concern and compassion to make a difference in the lives of the veterans residing in the facility. Your efforts to ensure their comfort and strength are worthy of the highest praise, for our veterans are the nation's greatest treasure and are to be celebrated and lauded for their sacrifices to safeguard our liberties.

You have striven to better the world around you by willingly spending time with many of the patients and families at the Hospice of the Western Reserve, and you have shown the potential of individuals to have a positive effect on society. Your generosity has earned you the respect and esteem of all who know you, and we are certain that you will continue to put forth the same unwavering commitment to excellence in your future endeavors.

Thus, it is with sincere pleasure that we commend you on your recent accolade and salute you as one of Ohio's finest citizens.

Senator Larry Obhof
President of the Ohio Senate

Senator John Eklund
18th Senatorial District

Senator Kenny Yuko
25th Senatorial District

STATE OF OHIO

Executive Department

OFFICE OF THE GOVERNOR

Columbus

RESOLUTION

WHEREAS, Robert E. Zonneville entered the Armed Forces in 1943 and served as a Staff Sergeant in Company H, 121st Infantry Regiment, 8th Infantry Division; and

WHEREAS, he served overseas from December 1943 until July 1945, and was wounded at St. Lo in July 1944 and wounded again in Northern France in September 1944. He participated in the campaigns of Normandy, Northern France, Rhineland, and Central Europe; and

WHEREAS, Mr. Zonneville is a recipient of the Bronze Star Medal, the Purple Heart Medal with Oak Leaf Cluster, the European-African-Middle Eastern Theater Ribbon with four battle stars, the Good Conduct Medal, the Combat Infantryman Badge, the Certificate of Merit, and three Overseas Service Bars; and

WHEREAS, his heroic actions in helping to liberate the French people have earned him one of the highest recognitions that France can bestow; and

WHEREAS, we owe the veterans of World War II an enormous debt of gratitude that can never be fully repaid.

NOW, THEREFORE, We, John R. Kasich and Mary Taylor, Governor and Lieutenant Governor of the State of Ohio, do join all citizens of Ohio to honor and thank

ROBERT E. ZONNEVILLE

on the occasion of the presentation to him of the Medal of Knight of the French Legion of Honor.

On this 6th day of December, 2013;

John R. Kasich
Governor

Mary Taylor
Lieutenant Governor

From Govenor Kasich

OHIO SENATE

HONORING ROBERT ZONNEVILLE
FOR EXEMPLARY ACCOMPLISHMENT

On behalf of the members of the Senate of the 128th General Assembly of Ohio, we are pleased to congratulate Robert Zonneville on being inducted into the 2010 Lake County Senior Citizens Hall of Fame.

The Lake County Senior Citizens Hall of Fame recognizes the contributions and achievements of older adults, and this prestigious honor is a fitting tribute to you for making a positive difference in your community. A decorated veteran of World War II and a retired employee and former chief executive officer of Landstar Systems, Inc., you have served in various capacities and conducted fundraisers for numerous organizations, including Hospice of the Western Reserve, the Mentor Senior Center, the Cardinal Cage Club, the American Legion, the Veterans of Foreign Wars, Mentor Civic Center and Euclid daycares, several homeowners associations, and Boulevard Presbyterian Church, and you have gone back to college to complete your business degree. You have combined civic concern and commitment with selfless initiative to become a dynamic local leader, and through your unwavering dedication to service, you have certainly distinguished yourself as a conscientious and hard-working Ohioan.

Your success is a justifiable source of pride and an excellent reflection not only on you but also on your family and your community. Over the years, you have earned the respect and admiration of many, and it is through the unceasing efforts of people such as you that the State of Ohio continues to grow and prosper and remains a pleasant place in which to live and work.

Thus, with sincere pleasure, we commend you on your recent accolade and salute you as one of Ohio's finest citizens.

Senator Bill Harris
President of the Ohio Senate

Senator Timothy Grendell
18th Senatorial District

Lake County Senior Hall of Fame

by Authority of

Secretary of State
Of Ohio

JON HUSTED
the 53rd Ohio Secretary of State

Robert E. Zonneville

It is my privilege to recognize Robert E. Zonneville for receiving the French National Order of the Legion of Honor.

This Certificate of Commendation is tendered on behalf of the people of the State of Ohio as a small token of their gratitude and sincere admiration. The accomplishments and consistent successes of Robert E. Zonneville are testaments to what can be done for the lives of others and for our communities. The deserved recognition is an inspiration to others for what they can achieve with similar, exemplary attitude, dedication and spirit.

Robert E. Zonneville entered military service in 1943 and served as a Staff Sergeant in Company H of the 121st Infantry Regiment of the 8th Division. From December 1943 to July 1945, he fought in Normandy, Northern France, Rhineland and Central Europe. In July of 1944, he was wounded in the fight to free the city of St. Lo. He was wounded again in the north of France in September 1944. He is the recipient of the Certificate of Merit, the Purple Heart Medal with Oak Leaf Cluster, the Bronze Star Medal, the Good Conduct Medal, the E.A.M.E. Theater Ribbon with four bronze battle stars, the Combat Infantryman Badge, as well as three Overseas Service Bars.

As Ohio's 53rd Secretary of State, it is my honor and unique distinction to commend Robert E. Zonneville for receiving the French Legion of Honor. May your good and honorable work stand as a measure for those who follow, inspiring them to believe in and work for the betterment of the lives of the people and communities throughout the State of Ohio.

Ohio Secretary of State
December 3, 2013

The Board of Trustees
Lakeland Community College
Lake County State of Ohio

Upon The recommendation of the Faculty has conferred upon
Robert E. Zonneville
the degree
Associate of Arts
With all Honors, Rights and Privileges appertaining to that degree.
In Witness Thereof, the undersigned have affixed their names
and the seal of Lakeland Community College.
Dated at Lake County, Ohio, this month of December, two thousand twelve

Chair, Board of Trustees — President — Executive Vice President and Provost and Dean of Faculty

Williamson Central High School

This Certifies That
Robert E. Zonneville
has completed the Course of Study prescribed by the Board of Education for the Williamson Central High School and is awarded this
DIPLOMA

Given at Williamson, New York, this 24th day of June, 1942.

Clerk of School Board — President of School Board
District Superintendent — Supervising Principal

Letters

If one is known by the lives he or she has affected, then I present evidence of what my Father has accomplished on this planet. Here is a compilation of letters my father has received over the years, and on the advent of his retirement, from folks just wanting to say 'thank you' for some small or large act of compassion on his part. They give you a glimpse into what he has meant to others throughout his life. Robert Zonneville was never a household name, he never had a lot of money, though he lived as if he swam in the stuff. He lived what is considered a normal life as an ordinary man. He accomplished more than many but less than some others. He raised his family, taught them what was important and hoped they would be happy in life. He didn't grumble when times were bad, but he celebrated life and lived it to its' fullest extent. He traveled, he saw the world, he met new friends and acquaintances every day, and sometimes he just kept the connection to humanity open.

If I have learned anything from my father, it is that, it is not always the high and mighty, the powerful and prodigious who influence our lives, who have the greatest impact. It is those we truly admire and respect, those we interact with every day, because of how they live their lives, what they contribute to a community and how their interactions affect those in their sphere; either directly or through others. Some influence our lives by kindness, giving, not judging but lending a supportive hand, how they treat all they meet. Some influence our lives as an example of what we don't want to be, how we don't wish to live our lives.

My father was never cruel. He very seldom laid a hand on us but when he did you knew you didn't want it to happen again. He could be harsh but always fair. Did he change the world? I would have to say emphatically, yes, yes, he did and the lives of all those he touched. Here is testament to that;

Dear Bob,

I just got off the phone with my son Dan in Santa Cruz. His best friend, teacher, mentor, musical associate and role model was just buried Thursday. The man was killed in a car crash in the prime of his life and career and Dan was not ready for this tragedy at all. He is reeling from the shock and as we talked I realized that I had meant to write this letter to you for at least 20 years now.

You are one of the major reasons for my success as human being on this planet. As a role model and mentor you gave me a foundation that I desperately needed during my lost years. As I began to mature and live my married life, I had you and Carol as my center of balance. Your family's commitment to and acceptance of each other gave me reference points to guide me on the path through the years. As messed up as I was, I still had your example to refer to and to give me hope of a better future.

Your energy and enthusiasm was a mystery to me. I have a natural negative outlook at life and I have lost many good opportunities through the years because I had no faith in the future. You gave me a spirit of hope in spite of myself. Your ability to go with the flow and keep your spirits up always inspired me to try to look at the bright side of things even though I was not particularly good at it.

I have wanted to write this for a long time but I was always afraid it would be real sappy and you would not respond to it well being that you are a pretty no nonsense kind of a guy. Anyway I feel really good about saying these things now because I am finally becoming the person that God intended me to be and a lot of my silly fears are being taken away. So like it or not here it is, I just Wanted to say thank you for believing in me and loving me and showing me a way to think and live and feel that helped me find God and peace in this life. You are my main man and I wanted to say it officially before andother 20 years or 20 minutes goes by and I didn't do it.

God bless you and your family and I hope to see you in July when we're in town for Justin Brock's wedding. Please don't hold it against me for being a little sappy!

Z

Love, Freddie Robbins

I was surprised my father kept this letter from Freddie because my father was never a sentimentalist as far as I knew. Learn something new every day! Here's another, one of many on his ultimate retirement;

Z,

I just wanted to drop you a note and thank you for all your support and guidance through the years. You have been a great influence in my life and many of the things that you have said and done, I have taken to heart. There are not many people like you in the world and I am proud to call you my friend. I will miss you dearly. Take care of yourself and I will look for those Xmas cards every year,

Love, Paula Deppe

I will not print all the letters he received, nor all that is contained in those letters, but a few examples are needed to show what he meant to his people, not just as a boss, but as a friend, confidant and mentor. So, here are a few more;

Dear Bob and Carol,

It's probably not 'politically correct' in a business sense, but, we love you guys. You two are such very special people, not just to the industry but to Wade and me personally. You bring such honor, dignity and trust to what, at times, a very difficult business. Solely because of you I've made it through some really bad times, in 'trucking'. Because of your strength, your encouragement and your guidance, we've made it.

Lyn and Wade Bourdon

Here is an oldie but a goodie on the advent of his 80th birthday;

Hello Bob,

I would be remiss if I didn't remember your 80th birthday. And, I am sorry to say that I didn't get to know you about 40 years ago. As you know, life brings us many blessings in the way of family, associates and friends. I can truly say that I have thoroughly appreciated your friendship although it has only been some three short years.

I value your friendship because I respect what you stand for as a man. I'm familiar with some of your extended efforts in charitable fund raising, generosity in showing others a good time and other compassionate efforts in reaching out to others. You are a giver in every sense of the word and I know beyond a show of a doubt that you expect nothing in return. Coupled with your true generosity and good will I see a very humble yet highly effective leader with character beyond reproach-a rare combination in today's environment.

Thanks Bob so very much for your friendship and our most sincere best wishes for a Happy 80th Birthday!!

Warm Regards,

George Kalivoda

In 1994 Inway/Landstar created an award for excellence, it encompasses impeccable values, commitment to family, respect from every peer and colleague and service to community. A commitment to excellence and safety in the trucking industry. The Robert E. Zonneville Lifetime Achievement Award, it is presented every year to the employee of the Landstar Group the exemplifies these qualities. Dad, of course, was the first recipient. Though it came as a complete surprise. They had kept the award and all information concerning its existence and to whom it was bound a secret up until its inaugural presentation. He was flabbergasted. From Bob Becker, Sales Manager;

Bob,
I was so pleased to have been present this year at the 1994 Landstar Convention when you received your award from Jeff Crowe. 'Z', no one deserves this award more than you. You not only made a great contribution to INWAY, but you also made a great contribution to the trucking industry. I am very proud not only to say that I know you and what you did for our industry but also to be able to say you were a good friend.

When your industry, as a whole, recognizes what you have accomplished and those who know you best are so kind in their assessment of, not only, your contribution to that industry but what you meant to them personally, I think that says a great deal about the person. Over 1,100 people attended this convention. In 2005 this became the Jeff Crowe/Robert Zonneville Award, my father was honored to share this yearly distinction with his good friend and compatriot.

My father was always willing to not just raise money or awareness for good causes and charities, he has also given of his time and himself, but also to be there for friends and those who worked for him and by his side.

He was presented an award from the Shriners, Al Koran Temple, for contributions to their $100 Million Dollar Club benefitting and covering the medical costs for crippled children in the Shriners Hospital Network.

In 1999 he took over fund raising and the golf outing for the Mentor High School Basketball team. The money raised goes to help provide shoes and equipment for the kids participating in the Mentor, Ohio basketball program. To date they have raised more than $100,000 for equipment and travel and the award is now named after my mother.

Though he was a registered Democrat most of his life he worked on the Voinovich For Governor campaign and he and mom attended the Inauguration in Columbus. I don't know if my father really looked at the D or R at the end of a candidate's name or just cared more about what they would do for the people. He may not have agreed with everything George Voinovich stood for, but he knew him to be a good man who served his community, either as Mayor, Governor or Senator, not his party. He always voted his heart and what he believed was best for his constituents, not what his political affiliation demanded of him. Dad was always particularly proud of his work on this campaign.

He is a Duke of Paducah and a Kentucky Colonel, in 2013 he was surprised by receiving the French Knight of the Legion of Honor medal.

Dear Mr. Zonneville,

It is a great honor and privilege to present you with the Knight of the Legion of Honor medal. Through this award, the French Government pays tribute to the soldiers who did so much for France and Western Europe. More than 65 years ago, you gave your youth to France and the French people. Many of you fellow soldiers did not return, but they remain in our hearts.

Thanks to your courage, and to our American friends and allies, France has been living in peace for the past six decades. You saved us and we will never forget. For us, the French People, you are heroes. Gratitude and remembrance are forever in our souls.

To show our eternal gratitude, the government of the French Republic has decided to award you the Legion of Honor. Created by Napoleon, it is the highest honor that France can bestow upon those who have achieved remarkable deeds for France.

Thank you for what you did and congratulations,
Graham Paul
Consul General de France

From President of Homeowners Associations, cocktail party skipper, President of INWAY, dockworker, truck driver, Regional Manager, vice President and Abraham Lincoln on a float. But I think if you asked him what he was most proud of, what title mean the most, it would be husband to Carol; Father to Betsy, Robin, Kim and David; Grandfather to Kathryn, Adrienne, Ellen, Greg and Jennifer; Brother to Duane, Richard and Allen; And friend to many. A word from dear friend Ed Blakemore;

Dear Bob and Carol,

I was sitting at my desk today thinking about this past weekend and trying to figure out just what is a friend. The dictionary says, 'a friend is a person whom one knows, likes and trusts.' My definition is just one word, 'Zonneville.'

You truly are two of the finest people I've ever known and, believe me, I have met many people in my life time. Lil will always remember her 50th birthday because of thoughtful people like you. We're so proud to know people like you and if prayer works we are going to be together for many more years.

Again, thanks for being so kind and always remember one thing,
We love you!

Ed and Lil Blakemore

There is no greater testament to anyone's life than the love, appreciation and honor given by friends and family. My father is the finest man I have ever known. My mother is the finest woman I have ever known. They are my inspiration and all I can aspire to, as they are the finest people I have ever known. And if there is one constant in his life, my father has never forgotten those whom he shared life and death with. He remembers those who stood shoulder to shoulder with him in France, Luxemburg, Belgium and Germany. Most years will find him on Memorial Day and Veterans Day at a National or local Cemetery speaking in their names;

Today we celebrate Memorial Day, originally called Decoration Day. We have but two days each year when we remember all those who answered the call when our nation needed us. One is Veteran Days, which is to remember and honor all living and deceased who served our country in war and peacetime. The other, is the day we are her for today. Memorial Day, whose purpose is to remember those who died in battle or as a result of injuries sustained in battle.

On Memorial Day we need to stop and pay with sincere conviction our respects for those who died protecting and preserving the freedoms we enjoy. For we owe those honored dead more than we can ever repay.

There are many stories as to the actual beginning of this day, but generally Waterloo, New York is considered where is started. Waterloo is a small town in central New York State. In 1865 the practice of decorating soldiers graves had become widespread in the north. The first known official observance was in Waterloo on May 5, 1866. On May 5, 1868, general John Logan, commander in Chief of the Grand Army of the Republic proclaimed Decoration Day should be observed on May 30th. It was called decoration Day because it was a day to decorate the graves of those killed or died because of injuries suffered in war. New York was the first state to officially recognize Decoration Day on 1873. By 1890 all Northern states had recognized it. The Southern states used different days depending on state. After World War I all states recognized May 30th.

In 1915, inspired by the poem, "In Flanders Fields", Monica Michael replied with her own poem;

We cherish the poppy red
That grows on fields where valor led,
It seems to signal to the skies
That blood of heroes never dies

She then conceived the idea to wear poppies on Memorial Day in honor of those who died serving their country. She was the first to wear one and sold poppies to her friends and co-workers with the money going to help needy service members. In 1922 the VFW was the first Veteran's organization to nationally sell poppies to help the needy.

It remained Decoration Day until after World War II when it was officially proclaimed to be Memorial Day.

Traditional observance of Memorial Day has diminished over the years.

We seem to have forgotten the solemnness and true meaning of this day.

In our history over one and a quarter million men and women have given their lives for our country and another two million have been wounded. For this type of sacrifice, we should be able to have a day to remember.

Rarely a day goes by that we do not hear about the national debt. I believe the debt we owe these heroes who made the supreme sacrifice is far greater than the national debt, and we only recognize it on Memorial Day. It is sad that we only remember them as a nation one day a year. With all the national cemeteries, both here and abroad, there is certainly no shortage of reminders.

While we remember those heroes today, we must never forget the sacrifices of the parents, wives and children of these fallen heroes. I cannot fathom what it must be like to lose someone in a far-off place, not really knowing much of what happened and when the remains will return. For those who have lost someone, well, the loneliness carries on for a very long time.

Surprisingly, we still have some fine Remembrances. Since the late 1950's the 3rd Infantry Division places small American flags on all the graves at Arlington national Cemetery. They then patrol the cemetery 24 hours a day, all weekend, to ensure those flags remain standing. There are many other places where Veteran's organizations and Boy and Girl Scouts also do this kindness. In 1951 the Boy and Cub Scouts of St. Louis began placing flags on the 150,000 graves at the Jefferson Barracks National Cemetery, a practice they continue to this day.

People of liberated countries sometimes show more of the true spirit of Memorial Day than we do here. For example, a 2001 U.S. Memorial Day guestbook entry from a citizen of the Netherlands;

In 1999 I laid flowers at the grave of a young U.S. fighter pilot who was killed in my village in 1945. In the Netherlands I know of schools adopting graves of allied servicemen, keeping those graves in excellent condition. Does anybody know of this happening in the United States?

A couple final comments;

Abraham Lincoln once said, "Gold is good in its place, but living, brave, patriotic men, are better than gold."

How to fly the flag on Memorial Day; It should be flown at half staff until noon and then flown full the balance of the day.

Great occasions do not make heroes or cowards. They simply unveil them to the eyes of men. Silently and imperceptibly, as we wake or sleep, we grow strong or week, and at last some crisis shows us what we have become. Brooke Foss Westcott

And just one more, if you don't mind;

Good Morning fellow Veterans and guests. We are here today celebrating Memorial Day, a day dedicated to those who gave their lives whiles serving our country.

I ask all Veterans to stand, if you can, or raise your hand. Here are a fe sobering numbers to show the tremendous sacrifices that have been mad;

WWII over 425, 000 lost their lives

Korea, more than 50,000

Vietnam over 58,000.

These are only three major conflicts. We have lost more brave men and women in Iraq and Afghanistan, there were more than 240 killed in one attack during the Reagan administration, and the numbers continue to grow. I mention these numbers because far too often we forget the cost in lives, and services such as this one today is a small price to pay for the sacrifice these people have made. One more statistic, the average life span today is a little over 76 for men and 81 for women. The average age for the above group was around 23. Quite a sobering set of numbers.

Today is also special for me as I get to publicly thank the students at All Saints Middle School in Wickliffe who came out here on May 9th and spent several hours cleaning the headstones and monuments, grave markers of Veterans. 140 students and 850 graves, this was a project All saints took on and several of us old Veterans come out to observe than thank them. To my knowledge this is a first of its kind.

Sometimes I hear comments that the people of Europe or Korea do not appreciate that we saved their countries. First off most of the time we were doing it to also save our own country, secondly I have visited the cemeteries of France, Belgium and Luxemburg. In many of these, since WWII, every grave has been adopted by either a person, family, school, business or other group. They place flowers on the adoptee grave on both Veterans Day and Memorial Day. Some even do this honor on the individuals birthday.

A few years ago the President of South Korea put together a beautiful book of what it was like when our troops were over there fighting and what it is like today. They shipped those books to the US to be distributed to Korean war Vets. I do not know of any projects, such as these, in the Untied States.

While wandering this cemetery on the 9th and seeing all the names of the Veterans, I felt a great sense of pride at being part of this small group called Veterans. I am sure in reading the names on the markers every nationality was here, every religion and every color. They all stood up for the U.S. when called upon.

In conclusion I think it would be nice if all of us urged our fellow citizens to postpone their barbeque, picnic or whatever until after lunch and take a few hour to come to this or any of the hundreds of National Cemeteries to remember these brave Veterans who stepped forward when called and gave their full measure. I hope we don't but fear we may need people like this again, as history has shown over and over again.

A few parting thoughts from my father and maybe a glimpse into why he feels it is so necessary to give back to those who gave all, to show our appreciation for what they gave, and try, with all we are capable of, to make this the country we want it to be. To make it, truly, the greatest country on earth. That's my dad. That is Robert Earl Zonneville. Hope you enjoyed meeting him, he's one hell of a guy.

Z

A Quick Genealogy for the Zonneville Clan

We have been able to go back to Adriaan Zonneville who was born in Biervliet, Holland on October 3, 1815. He married Suzanne Boone who had been born in Hoofdplaat, Holland on June 13, 1824 though we do not have the date of the marriage we do know they had 11 children, 9 of whom survived past infancy.

Johanna was born March 5, 1842

Jacobus Adriaan was also born in Hoofdplaat, as were all the Zonneville children from this marriage, on July 20, 1846, like many of the children born at this time they have been lost to time and we don't know much about them if anything at all.

Suzanna was born February 12, 1850

Wilhelmina was born November 27, 1860

Isaac was born January 19 1863 and apparently died young as the next child was also named Isaac Martinus born February 27, 1864

Adriaan Jacobus came along on May 3, 1865 followed by Catharina on April 13, 1866

Martinus Johannus our great grandfather was born on May 5, 1867 he is followed by Pieternella Suzanna on august 31, 1868 and Catharina Pieternella on June 5, 1870 making one wonder how many of these children lived as the names seem to continue in differing incarnations through the years tying the family to their past. The family seemed to remember the children lost by naming the next child or so in their honor

Martinus married Suzanna Hendrika DeBatz of Schoondijke she was born in 1869. They had six children four of whom survived infancy, one who later died in early childhood. They were Jacob A. born in Schoondijke on December 28, 1887; Suzanna C. Born Schoondijke on January 10, 1891 and died in infancy; Suzanna C. born in Schoondijke March 21, 1894, also died in infancy; Adrian J. born Schoondijke on January 2, 1898; Isaac A. born Schoondijke January 24, 1903 and Suzanna C. born Schoondijke June 30, 1904, she died at two and half years old after arriving in America. . Suzanna died in Williamsno on October 6, 1946. Martinus died in Williamson November 21, 1947

Jacob Adrian Zonneville married Katie Tellier, born Oostburg, Holland in

1889, on December 2, 1909 they had five children; Martin Jake born Williamson April 28, 1911; John Martin born Williamson December 8, 1913 died in infancy; Isaac John born Williamson October 21, 1915; Anna Susan born Williamson September 14, 1918; John Jacob born Williamson December 1, 1919. Jacob passed in 1964

Adrian Jacob, our grandfather Married Mattie Leona Shippers on March 22, 1922. Mattie was the daughter of Jacob shippers and Jennie Peterham. She was born in 1902 and died June 17, 1952. They had seven children, four of whom survived into adulthood. Evelyn Jean was born in Williamson July 13, 1922, she died on February 7, 1923; Robert Earl was born in Williamson on January 23, 1925; Duane was born in Williamson May 29, 1926; Muriel Ruth was born in Williamson January 27, 1928 and died May 26 of the same year; Richard was born November 2, 1931; Allen was born October 7, 1932; And Gerald came along on December 3, 1935 and died on January 16, 1936.

Robert married Carol Alliger on June 7, 1947 they had four children Bethann born 1949 and Married to Robert Schulz; Robin born January 1952 and married to Manette Reebel; Kim born 1953 and married Robin Stratton July 12, 1975, divorced April 1983, married Nancy on October 27, 1984; David born 1956 married Clarissa in 1976, divorced mid-80's, married Cindy in 1995.

Betsy and Bob have two children, Ellen born in 1979 and Gregory born in 1981;

Ellen is now married to Matt Kohn between them they have four children;

Steven Jack Geiger born on 03
Cristian James born in 07
Isabella Frances born in 09
Madison Kohn Born in 2010
Gregory and Jessica now have a lovely brood for three children;
Jackson Robert born in 2011
Samuel Thomas born in 2014
Madeleine Ann born in 2017

Robin and Manette have the green bean queen, Jennifer Reebel born in 1980

She has the one son AJ, Allen Joseph, born in 2013

Kim and Robin Stratton had two children;
Kathryn born in 1975
She Married Jim Corrigan in 2003
Adrienne born in 1977
David and Cindy have had a series of dogs and cats

Duane and Virginia had one son, Charlie, born 1956, he is married to the lovely Donna, born 1957, they have a passel of children;
Adam (Adam Charles) 1981

Married to Megan (Megan Cole) 1982
Abram Charles 2011
Aurora Joleigh 2013

Adrienne (Adrienne Marie Nolan)1983
Married to Matt (Matthew Nolan) 1981
Isabelle (Isabelle Grace Nolan) 2011
Emmett (Emmett Michael Nolan) 2013

Amanda (Amanda Leigh Tilburg) 1987
Married to Ryan (Ryan Tilburg) 1985

Olivia (Olivia Marie Tilburg) 2015
Madelyn (Madelyn Leigh Tilburg) 2017

Alyssa (Alyssa Michelle Zonneville) 1991
Cameron (Cameron Bodine) 1990
Alyssa and Cameron are getting married on September 15, 2018

Richard and Martha unleashed four girls upon this planet;
Annie was born in 1959 and passed away from cancer in 1995
Sandy was born in 1960 she has three daughters;
Victoria born 1988(?)
Katelyn (1990?) she has a daughter Lucy born April of 2017
Breanne (1998?)
Penny was born in 1965(?)
And Susan was born in 1970(?) and has two daughters, Elizabeth and Leslie

Allen married Nancy and they had two children Lori and Jeff
Lori was born in 1958 and has four sons;
Jason Allen Montgomery born 1980 and married to Ashley Cogdill they have a daughter Reese Bea born
2011
Grayson Dill born 2013
Nicholas David born 1981 and married to Erin Clark
Brett Thomas MeCullough born 1990 and has a daughter Riley Marie born in 2012
Jeff has four children, three by Deborah Kay, sorry do not know the name of his second wife. Deborah married a wonderful man it has been a pleasure to get to know, Robert Black in August 2002
Dana Brown born 1981 married to Dustin August 2008 they have two children Keegan born 2010 and Logan born 2015
Jerica Paige Stroud born 1986 and is now married to Steven Stroud he

has a son Owen

Twin daughters Ava Louise and Evelyn Kay 2019
Jonathon Blaine Zonneville born 1987
Married Mary Liles May 19, 2021
Daughter Jacqueline Faith 2022

That is the family I know of. They are all loud, argumentative, fun, drink, laugh and are a joy to know and I am so proud they are my family. Thank you to the Zonnevilles who made the cold, hard trek from Holland to give us all this wonderful opportunity!

I have not included complete birthdays out of paranoia for the times in which we live. If anyone in the family would like more complete data, just contact me and I will share. Sorry, the news and Facebook make me worried.

ABOUT THE AUTHOR

K. Adrian Zonneville is a Singer/Songwriter and Professional Comedian and has toured the country for the past 45 years. He has performed in 49 states, Canada, Ireland and Key West. He has previously written one book, American Stories. He lives with his wife of over 30 years and a lovely Bearded-Collie, Greta. His two daughters have kindly moved out and are doing quite nicely on their own.

His book, American Stories, is available at all fine online retailers as an eBook or as a real life, hold in your hand book.

To find out more please check out the links below;

To connect on Facebook;
https://www.facebook.com/KAdrianZonneville/

For Twitter; https://twitter.com/KAZonneville

Or check out the performer side of me at; www.charliewiener.com

Made in the USA
Middletown, DE
12 April 2022